Charlene Shea

ABSOLUTELY

ABSOLUTELY
YOU CAN CREATE POSITIVE LIFE CHANGES

By

Charlene Shea

with

Joanne Wilkens

To my fantastic family that continues to say,
"Absolutely! You can do it"

TABLE OF CONTENTS

ACKNOWLEDGMENTS   X

ABOUT THE AUTHORS   XI

PREFACE   1

1 THE CHALLENGE OF SELF-LOVE   5

   WHY SELF-LOVE IS DIFFICULT   5
   BEYOND YOUR SHADOW SELF   6
   BREAKING THE BARRIER OF SELF-DOUBT   8
   CHANGE YOUR NEGATIVE MIND   11
   WHY SELF-LOVE IS IMPORTANT   11
   THE SECRET OF SELF-LOVE   14
   THREE STEPS TO POSITIVE SELF-DIALOGUE   15

2 MAKE A COMMITMENT TO CHANGE   19

   FROM WELFARE MOTHER TO TV PERSONALITY   20
   UNDERSTANDING THE CHANGE PROCESS   23
   DISCOVERING THE PRINCIPLE OF CHANGE   25
   THE PRINCIPLE OF CHANGE: PRACTICAL APPLICATION   26
   RESISTANCE TO CHANGE   27
   WHY CHANGE IS DIFFICULT   30
   THE THREE BARRIERS TO CHANGE   32
   CONCLUSION   39

3 VISUALIZE YOUR PERFECT LIFE   43

   THE POWER OF THE MIND   45

BARRIERS TO VISUALIZATION   46
MINDPOWER ON THE SLOPES   54
BELIEVE AND ACHIEVE: VISUALIZING LIFE CHANGE   56

4   ON YOUR MARK, GET SET, GOALS!   60

TWO HOURS TO LIVE   62
THERE'S ALWAYS HOPE   62
AWAKE AND AWARE   63
I CAN AND I WILL   65
HOME AGAIN, HOME AGAIN   66
GOING THE DISTANCE STEP BY STEP   67
FROM VISUALIZATION TO GOAL SETTING   68
BECOMING A WINNER   72

5   COUNT YOUR STRENGTHS   79

D—DOMINANCE   82
I—INFLUENCING OF OTHERS   83
S—STEADINESS   84
C—COMPLIANCE (TO THEIR STANDARDS)   85
THE FOUR STYLES: A SUMMARY   87
THE FOUR STYLES: NEEDS AND MOTIVATION   88
COUNT YOUR STRENGTHS   91
STRENGTHS INTO WEAKNESS   94
DISC—SELF ANALYSIS   95

6   VICTORY OVER FEAR   97

YOUR CAPACITY FOR RISK   99
DIFFERENT STYLES, DIFFERENT ATTITUDES   101
ASSESS THE RISK FACTORS   102
FINDING THE COURAGE WITHIN   103

JUST AN AVERAGE GUY   104
MANAGING UNCERTAINTY   108
Think Positively   110
MOMENT TO MOMENT   112
HELLO/GOOD-BYE   113
DELIVER THE LETTER   114

7   WHAT ELSE DO I NEED TO DO   **116**

    PROJECTING CONFIDENCE: TEN CRITICAL SKILLS   119

8   BLUEPRINT FOR CHANGE   **129**

    CONCLUSION   135

    BIBLIOGRAPHY   **136**

ACKNOWLEDGMENTS

We wish to thank Edward Bernstine, Denise Codgen, Sylvio Dupuis, Katherine Ferrans, Donna Rafdal, Florence Shepherd, Wendy Wilkens and Dottye Yakovakis for reading and commenting on the book at various stages of its development. Their suggestions and support were invaluable to us. We also thank Valerie Zabella for her heroic efforts in computerizing the manuscript. We extend our deepest gratitude to all the interviewees who shared their inspirational stories with us. We learned important lessons from their experiences as we hope you will, too. Finally, we thank our families and friends for their love and encouragement. Without their help and good cheer, this project would have been infinitely more difficult.

We believe this book represents the best that a collaborative effort can produce. Working together has been a rewarding and fruitful experience for both of us. It has brought us deeper clarification of our ideas, expanded professional development, friendship and this book. We acknowledge one another for these productive results.

ABOUT THE AUTHORS

Charlene Shea, CSP is a nationally known speaker and seminar leader who has inspired hundreds of people to create positive life changes. A graduate of the University of Maine, she lived and taught abroad before starting her own speaking and seminar business in 1980. The focus of her work since then has been on human relations. She received the designation Certified Speaking Professional from the National Speakers Association. She is listed in Who's Who in American Women and Who's Who in World Women. Absolutely! is her first book. It represents a synthesis of the ideas she has developed over the past thirty years to help people in diverse fields achieve their dreams. Mother of three grown children and a grandmother of two, she lives in New Hampshire with her husband.

Joanne Wilkens is a freelance writer who lives and works in New Hampshire. Her first book, Her Own Business: Success Secrets of Entrepreneurial Women, was published by McGraw-Hill. A graduate of Goucher College, she holds an M.A. from the University of California, Berkeley. She has taught English and writing at various California and Eastern colleges and is currently working on a book about the history of science. She has two sons.

PREFACE

In August, 1989 I saw a new decade fast approaching. The start of the 1990s would coincide with the finish of my first ten years in business—ten exhilarating years of growth and development. As I looked back over what I had accomplished, I realized that I had fulfilled many of my life dreams. I also realized that I had relied on a very powerful inner process to guide me to success. This book is the result of those two realizations.

Even as a child, I was told I had a good imagination because I could see myself doing things I had never done before. I was also encouraged to pursue what I loved to do most: speaking before a group. All during my childhood and through college, I took advantage of every possible opportunity to talk to people in public. Whenever I addressed a new group or discussed a more difficult topic, I was always scared, yet I learned to see myself meeting each new challenge successfully and then to act as if that vision of my success were absolutely true.

I have followed this same principle all my life. I visualized what I was going to accomplish, set goals for myself to reach, and then set out to achieve them. No matter what fears I had or obstacles I faced, I kept moving toward my goal. My guiding vision always enabled me to act with confidence and self-belief because I knew I was doing what was right for my life. Sometimes I was scared, at times I met barriers I did not expect. However, I still kept moving toward my goal.

The more I worked with other people, the more I realized how powerful my personal process was. Over the years I shared this process in my seminars and workshops, and the participants responded with tremendous enthusiasm. Many asked me to write up what I was teaching in book form so they

1

could have something concrete to take home. The handouts and worksheets that I had prepared simply did not meet their needs. Yet the more they asked, the more resistance I felt. Writing had never been my strength, and I could not face the blank page. Although I strongly believed in my ideas, I was unable to write them down.

Even while my mother encouraged me to speak, she sharply criticized my writing. One of my old childhood tapes goes something like this: "You're a terrific speaker and really can capture a group, but you sure can't write." My mother not only read all my essays but rewrote them as well. My old tapes, combined with my natural disinclination to sit alone before a computer screen, kept my book from becoming a reality.

Several years ago, I met a man who assured me he could get my ideas down on paper quickly and effectively. His offer sounded like the perfect solution to my problem. I gave him all my materials, and a few weeks later he returned a disappointing manuscript. I felt very discouraged because what he had written simply was not me.

I had envisioned myself with a book, but perhaps I needed to think my goals through more carefully. Why did I want a book? What purpose would it serve in my life? How important was it for me to do this? Whom would my book help and what messages did I really want to communicate? What was my focus, my style, my voice? I realized that once I answered these questions, I would find the right way to proceed.

In July, 1989 I met a man at the National Speakers Association who was proudly signing copies of his new book. By now, I had thought my own project through more carefully, so I asked him how he had ever managed to get his book done. He told me he had advertised for a co-author, interviewed several people, read their work carefully and chosen the one he felt most suited to meet his needs. His advice to me was to do the same.

The process sounded so simple. Why had I not thought of it before? I realized that, until this very moment, I had simply not been clear about my purpose or my goals. Now I was ready. When I returned home, I advertised in the local papers and was overwhelmed by the response. More than twenty-five people answered my ad, and I interviewed six. That is the story of how I met Joanne Wilkens. Neither of us could have foreseen the wonderful working relationship we would have and the mutual benefits we would gain from our association.

August, 1989 was a turning point for Joanne as well as for me. In 1989 she also made an important life decision to fulfill a long-held dream by writing her first book. Much as I had loved speaking, Joanne had always loved to write. Yet both of us had married young, had children, travelled with our husbands, worked in the field of education, and deferred doing what we really wanted to do the most. During the 1980s, both of us had been active in the feminist movement, and we both had followed a similar inner process and made a similar life change.

Joanne has spent the past decade becoming a writer much as I have worked to become a speaker. She researched and wrote a book on women entrepreneurs, and her book, Her Own Business: Success Secrets of Entrepreneurial Women, was published by McGraw-Hill in 1987. When Her Own Business was released, Joanne was determined to travel, speak, teach, organize or do whatever was necessary to make it successful. However, she found out that she was trying to do something that was not correct for her life.

Much as I am not a writer, Joanne is not a speaker. Although she achieved some success publicizing her book, she was very unhappy out in the public eye. Research, writing and working alone were what she liked to do best. So, when her youngest son graduated from high school, she made a

3

radical life change. She sold her home in California, left her job and a twelve-year relationship, and returned home to New Hampshire. She was determined to live where she felt happiest and find productive work writing.

Joanne was one of the twenty-five people who answered my call for writers. After meeting her and reading her book, I realized that we shared the same point of view as well as many experiences. Both of us live by and believe in the processes we have written about here. By following these processes ourselves, we met one another and achieved a new life goal. Together, we produced this book.

We hope that the information you find on the following pages will be as helpful to you as it has been to us. Since personal growth is an ongoing challenge, we often reread what we have written. We know that developing self-confidence is not easy, so we practice the three A's—acceptance, approval and appreciation—regularly. (See Chapter One.) We, too, feel scared when we initiate new projects and set out on new trails. However, we have learned that by visualizing a positive outcome and focusing on that vision, we can overcome almost any obstacle and reach our goals. (See Chapters Three and Four.) And we know how easy it is to fall into negative thinking and beliefs. The suggestions we make for developing a positive, goal-oriented outlook are ones we use on a regular basis. (See Chapters Two and Six.)

The exercises that we have provided offer practical steps to help you reach specific goals. They are not intended to help you solve deep inner conflicts or severe emotional problems. Such issues need to be discussed with a professional counselor or therapist.

We wish you the best as you journey through these pages. May you break your own personal barriers and achieve your life dream.

CHAPTER ONE

THE CHALLENGE
OF SELF-LOVE

My best friend is the person who
brings out the best in me.
– Henry Ford

Who is your best friend, the person who brings out the best in you? Your spouse, brother or sister? Your college roommate, football teammate, poker buddy or professional colleague? Any one of these people may be a close, supportive person in your life, a person who shares your secrets, encourages your aspirations and supports your dreams. However, the most important friend you will ever have is the one person who will never leave your side: yourself. Yet few people dream of including themselves on their list of best friends. Why is this?

WHY SELF-LOVE IS DIFFICULT

People everywhere suffer from a common and highly destructive condition: lack of self-love. It is a condition that is totally curable yet one that often lingers on for years, causing depression, unhappiness, frustration and immobility.

Lack of self-love prevents people from fully loving others, from accepting love in return, from succeeding in their work and from having the happiness that is there before them. It also prevents them from becoming their own best friends.

The process of developing self-love begins at birth. Children's feelings of worthiness and self-control start with a parent's response to their smiles and tears. Neglected babies start feeling unworthy, unlovable and unable to control their environment if their parents do not respond to their needy cries. During the toddler years, children continue absorbing both verbal and nonverbal messages about their self-worth. When they repeatedly hear comments such as, "You're too fat, too thin, too lazy, no good, not smart enough . . . , " they internalize these messages, which then become part of their self-image.

The picture of self that is formed during childhood is the one people carry with them in later life no matter how distorted it may be. Then, during their adult years, they behave according to what the picture tells them, as if it were absolutely accurate and true. Most of the time, this picture is not true at all, but as the basis of an individual's self-perception, it becomes a powerful determinant of adult behavior. Such internalized pictures are commonly called old tapes, scripts or movies, and–like real tapes, scripts, and movies–they can be changed. They are no more permanent than chalk drawings, and, together with other childhood lessons, can be erased from the blackboard of the mind. The first step to making this change is to accept the challenge of self-love.

BEYOND YOUR SHADOW SELF

Back in the 4th century B.C., the Greek philosopher, Plato, wrote about a group of people who lived in a dark cave deep within the earth. No sun penetrated their subterranean home, and fire was their only source of light. Bound by chains since early childhood, the cave dwellers stood immobile, their backs to the flame. In this vague, dim world they were unable to see clearly but rather perceived everything, including themselves, as shadowy forms cast on the wall opposite the fire. Because they had never seen anything in a different light, they accepted these shadowy forms as reality. Imagine their amazement when, one day, they emerged from their cave into the sunlight and saw the world in all its beauty and complexity. Momentarily dazzled by the brilliance of the sun, they cried out in wonder and pain.

Most of us are no different from Plato's cave-dwellers. We see only a shadow of our true selves because we focus on our weaknesses and shortcomings. Chained to our old tapes, scripts and negative self-messages, we are afraid to step out into the bright light for fear of seeing even more imperfections. However, when those early cavemen and women left their dark abode, they were dazzled not by Earth's ugliness and defects but by her beauty and perfection. As part of Earth's creation, each one of us shares in nature's glory. The problem is not a lack of beauty but our determination to accept a shadowy version of ourselves instead of the true reality of our being.

This chapter will enable you to be your own best friend by helping you find and express the very best in yourself. It will guide you out of the darkness of self-reproach and into the light of self-love. On the following pages, you will meet several people who have broken the barrier of self-doubt thereby changing their lives. You will learn why self-love is important and how to increase your feelings of self-worth. As you work through the processes offered here, you, like Plato's cave-dwellers, may feel awestruck and frightened. You may also experience pain. However, you have the power within you to break these inner barriers, to face your fears, overcome your doubts and become the person you want to be.

BREAKING THE BARRIER OF SELF-DOUBT

Changing your self-image and developing self-love requires you to change your thinking. It demands that you replace negative tapes and movies about yourself with positive ones. Your mind can hold only one thought at a time, so, when thinking about yourself, make sure this thought is favorable. In fact, do not permit harsh self-criticism to enter your mind. Remember, God never took time to make a nobody. You are a unique and perfect individual. In fact, you are the only and the most perfect version of YOU that exists. With effort and determination, you can replace your self-doubts with a positive self-vision. Martha Easton, a young advertising account executive, accepted this challenge and, by doing so, saved her own life.

When I first met Martha, she was a junior in college and a participant in one of my workshops. Today, she is twenty-six and already has achieved recognition in her field. Martha works for a prestigious Los Angeles advertising agency where she is admired by her co-workers and respected by her boss. Her clever, witty advertising campaigns have earned her several important accounts. Martha knows that she is a creative and dedicated professional, and she does not forget to congratulate herself every day for her achievements. She well remembers a time only a few years ago when self-congratulation was hardly a part of her daily routine. At that time, Martha suffered from a severe lack of self-esteem. Cut off from her own love and affection, she had little confidence and believed she had no control over her life.

Martha and I met when she attended my workshop series "Who Am I, Where Am I Going?" The other participants

8

were shocked when this beautiful, clever young woman shared her story. No one would ever have guessed the burden and pain she carried within her nor that her slim figure was testimony to her recent recovery from a long struggle with anorexia. Here is the story she told our group.

"I am the youngest of three children," she declared. "My sister, Jean, is the oldest and my brother, Paul, the middle child. Although that is supposed to be the 'difficult' position, I always believed Paul had it the best--the only son sandwiched between two sisters. From my point of view, he was very charming, a great athlete, everything a son should be, and my parents' favorite. My sister was very smart. She got straight A's in school, and as the oldest she always had a special aura of authority about her. For some reason, I always felt that in comparison to Jean and Paul, I just didn't measure up. As the baby of the family, I felt that no one took me seriously.

"By the time Jean was in high school, she had a tendency to gain weight, a tendency she never really overcame. Somehow in my mind, I believed that if I couldn't be as smart as she was I could certainly be thinner, and I just stopped eating. I also had a boyfriend who was very controlling. He bought me expensive gifts, but then tried to make me feel guilty every time I wanted to do something on my own, and I let him get away with it. Later, when I was in therapy, I realized that I had given up control of my life to my brother, my sister, my boyfriend. The only thing I felt I could decide for myself was whether or not I would eat.

"I went from a size 8 to a size 0 and hardly even noticed the difference, but that got me plenty of attention from my parents. Jean's academic record and Paul's football games suddenly were less important, and I became the center of everybody's concern. But I still didn't realize how serious the problem had become. Then one day I found myself in the children's section of a department store looking for a dress that would fit me. I was shocked! When I got home, I went and looked at myself in the bathroom mirror, I mean I REALLY looked at myself. I had just turned 18 and had my whole life ahead of me, and what I saw was terrible: thin parchment skin stretched tight over my stick-like bones. My first thought was almost funny: I looked like an advertisement for a Halloween skeleton costume!

"The next day I happened to see an advertisement on TV, one of those public service things telling about a local clinic that helps people with bulimia and anorexia. I was terrified that I was going to die, and deep down inside I knew that my life was worth saving, that I didn't want to starve myself to death. So I called the number given in the ad, and the next week had an appointment with a counselor. At that moment my life started to change because I decided that I had to do something about my situation or I would die. I stopped blaming my family and my boyfriend for what had happened to me, and started taking responsibility for changing my feelings and my behavior."

Martha spent the next year with a therapist she described as "the most understanding, yet toughest person I've ever known." She also attended group counseling sessions and did lots of reading on her own. Martha came to my workshops, where the emphasis was on developing self-confidence and a life plan, as part of her recovery program. By that time, she was a student at the state university and ready for some practical guidance on how to plan for a happy and productive future.

The day Martha Easton looked in the mirror and really noticed her body, she made a critical decision: to take control of her life. For Martha, the first step in the process was to seek professional help. With persistence and a real desire to change, she learned to be her own best friend. She grew to like and accept herself, and she stopped looking to other people for approval. Instead of focusing on her weaknesses, especially in contrast to her brother's and sister's strengths, she stopped comparing herself to them altogether. She realized that in such a comparison she always emerged the loser.

CHANGE YOUR NEGATIVE MIND

I used to start my motivation workshops by asking people what they wanted to change in themselves or their lives, and I could hardly stop the flow of ideas. Like Martha Easton, each person had little trouble listing the many negative attributes he or she wanted to change. However, I soon realized that starting on a negative note did not set the tone I wanted for the day's exercises and discussion. So I began asking participants to look at me and say something positive about themselves. Their responses were astonishing: a nervous laugh, downcast eyes, negative phrases, fidgeting, doodling and blushing. It was almost impossible to elicit a positive comment no matter who the people were, where they were from, what their ages, backgrounds, jobs or gender.

Most people learn to avoid talking positively about themselves at an early age. Such talk is generally viewed with disapproval. Parents regard it as boasting, other children call it bragging, our culture labels it conceit. Our conditioning in this area is so strong that when we reach adulthood, we are almost totally unable to compliment ourselves--either in public or in private. At times we are even unable to receive compliments from others. Breaking the barrier of self-doubt thus requires that we not only erase our internalized negative tapes but also reverse our social and cultural conditioning. We can do this best by learning to accept and love ourselves for who we are.

WHY SELF-LOVE IS IMPORTANT

People who like and are comfortable with themselves

11

project a positive self-image. They stand and move with confidence, and speak with clarity and forcefulness. Such people tend to be flexible, willing to listen to others and capable of bringing out the best in those around them. Self-acceptance lends an aura of authority to their words and actions; other people feel this aura and respond with acceptance and approval thereby generating a positive cycle of interaction. Self-love provides the foundation for inner security, forms the basis for assertive behavior and enables us to establish trusting relationships with other people. For all of us, learning to love ourselves is thus the first step to achieving control over our lives. The importance of this lesson is clear from the story of Cecile and Charles Connor, whose daughter, Susan, has Down's Syndrome.

The Connors attended a workshop I presented for the New Hampshire Department of Mental Health and Developmental Services. The audience, almost entirely parents of developmentally disabled children and adults, shared many inspiring stories; however, that told by Cecile Connor was particularly compelling.

"When our daughter was nine months old," Cecile Connor told the group, "she was diagnosed as a child who had Down's Syndrome. At that time, due to our persistent questioning, our family physician finally told us of her disability. Although he did not give us much information about the expectations for her development, we parented in the best way we could. When Susan was three, she was still not walking or talking. It was recommended that we have her development evaluated at a child guidance clinic. When we reviewed the report with a clinician, she said that we might want to consider an institutional setting for our daughter. For both Charles and me, that simply was not an option. I was brought up to believe that when you have a child, you are responsible for that child. I never could have sent Susan

12

away to be cared for by someone else. I also believed in her capacity to learn and grow in her own way and to become the adult she was meant to be.

"Charles and I decided that we were not going to impose any limits on our daughter, that we would help her become everything and anything that she could become. The first step in doing this was to build her confidence and teach her to accept herself. We knew that this would enable her to interact positively with other people and to try new experiences. How a family relates to any child, including a child who has Down's Syndrome, sets the tone for how others will relate to that child and how the child will relate to him or herself. We never wanted her to feel bad about herself or to think that she couldn't at least try something that interested her.

"By the time she was five, Susan was studying ballet to improve her coordination and taking piano lessons to develop strength in her hands. She attended a regular school with students of mixed ability, and later she became a Girl Scout, the only girl in the troop with a disability. Of course she experienced moments of rejection and frustration, but throughout everything we encouraged her to feel good about herself. To me, developing confidence and self-esteem is the most important thing any of us can do. We helped Susan do this by focusing on the things she could do, on her successes rather than on her failures."

Today, Susan Connor is thirty years old. She has part-time employment in Concord, New Hampshire doing office work and some data processing, and she is looking forward to increasing her hours. One of her leisure activities is attending jazzercise classes in her community. Thanks to the vision and belief of her parents, Susan is an independent adult who learned to be her own best friend. This achievement was facilitated by her parents' positive attitude; however, it is a one that each of us can master alone at any stage in our lives.

THE SECRET OF SELF-LOVE

All of us want what I call the 3 A's: approval, acceptance and appreciation, and we look desperately to other people to fulfill these needs. As a result, we behave in such a way as to elicit approval, acceptance or appreciation from those around us. We want our spouses to assure us we are smart and attractive, our bosses to tell us we are invaluable, our friends to note our loyalty, wit or concern. However, the more we expect and want these things from other people, the more we feel controlled by what other people do and say. We become devastated by the withholding of compliments, reassurance and affection, and our already shaky self-esteem becomes further eroded. We then become demanding in our relationships, insecure in our work and controlling in our behavior. How can you break this vicious cycle?

Learning to love yourself is the first step you must take. The more you are able to accept, appreciate and approve of yourself, the greater your personal freedom will be, and the better you will be able to achieve your dreams. No longer will you feel dependent on other people to provide the love you need to flourish and grow. Instead, you will always carry the source of that love within. Once this occurs, your confidence will increase and your self-doubts disappear. You then will be able to offer approval, acceptance and appreciation to others, and they in return will give them back to you, thereby creating a highly positive cycle.

The following three-step process will help you generate the three A's for yourself. It will also enable you to replace negative thought patterns about yourself with positive self-dialogue. The process is simple but, for most people, not easy. Do each step completely before moving on to the next.

14

THREE STEPS TO POSITIVE SELF-DIALOGUE

Step One. Accept Your Physical Self

Stand in front of the mirror completely nude and accept yourself the way you are. Look at the different parts of your body, including your scars and your flaws, and say, "I accept you the way you are." After you have done this exercise several times, answer the following questions when you are standing alone.

1. Note the expression on your face. Are you smiling?

2. What is the tone of your voice? Are you angry, critical, loving?

3. What part of you is most lovable? least lovable? Why?

4. What has your body done for you that you appreciate?

5. How can you show your body more acceptance, appreciation and approval?

Step Two. Approve of Your Personal Qualities

This exercise will help you express positive feelings about who you are as a person. Fill in the blanks with 10 positive statements about your personality, your abilities, your behavior. For example, you might start with "I like my open, friendly manner...I like my clever wit...I like the fact that I am working to change my life."

1._____

2._____

3._____

4._____

5._____

6._____

7._____

8._____

9._____

10._____

Now take your completed list, stand in front of a mirror, look at yourself and speak each item aloud. Smile at yourself and maintain good eye contact. Acknowledge each compliment either verbally or nonverbally, e.g., say "Thank you" to yourself, expand on the compliment, smile, wink, pat yourself on the back. Practice this dialogue every day, especially if you feel rejected, hurt or disappointed in yourself. Add new things to the list. Finally, expand your self-dialogue to actual conversation with another person. Tell your spouse, children, friends, boss something from your list.

Step Three. Appreciate Your Achievements

The following exercise will help you build self-appreciation through boasting about your most outstanding accomplishments. Answer the following questions as completely as you can. Note details wherever possible to support your answers.

1. What natural abilities do you have? What accomplishments have these abilities enabled you to achieve?

2. What things do you do better than most people?

3. How have you grown in the last year?

4. What are the most difficult or challenging things you have accomplished? Why were these things difficult for you? What things within yourself enabled you to accomplish them?

5. What accomplishments are you proudest of? Why?

6. What compliments about yourself would you most like to receive?

The challenge of self-love is open to everyone. Like Martha Easton, you can choose to end your diet of negativity and self-criticism and start nourishing yourself with acceptance, approval and appreciation. You can choose, as did Cecile Connor, to remove self-doubt and hesitation from your life path, thereby opening new doors for yourself as she opened them for her daughter, Susan. You can choose to take control of your circumstances and think positively about your appearance, abilities and accomplishments. Accepting this challenge is the first step in the process of self-change.

I accept this challenge.

_____   _____

Name   Date

CHAPTER TWO

MAKE A COMMITMENT TO CHANGE

Ring out the old, ring in the new.
– Alfred, Lord Tennyson

At least once a year, most of us turn inward for a moment and take a brief survey of our lives. For some people, that moment occurs on their birthday; for others, New Year's Day is a time of reflection and self-examination; for still others, a significant event triggers an unexpected life review. For many of you, choosing to read this book marked the moment you set out to examine the course of your life. One result of such self-investigation is a decision to change–to let go of the past and welcome the future, to say goodbye to those things you no longer want and to greet something fresh and different–be it a job, a relationship, a house, a car or new attitudes and beliefs about yourself and your situation. During this positive moment, you gladly ring out the old and ring in the new with all its potential for transforming your lives.

However, the decision to change is sometimes accompanied by uneasiness and doubt. Change requires us to alter our self-perception, to encounter something we have

19

never encountered before, to see and feel something totally new, to take responsibility for our lives. It demands that we break away from our standard routine and face the unknown. For many of us, this is surprisingly difficult to do.

To navigate successfully through unexplored waters, we need only rely on ourselves and our ability to choose the best course. Every one of us has the appropriate skills and life experiences to help us find the way, yet few of us trust our inner guide. When we lack confidence, it is difficult for us to face change without anxiety and fear. Although our desire for self-transformation may be great, our desire to avoid unknown emotions is greater still. As a result, we remain in unproductive, unhappy situations for years, adapting to familiar discomfort rather than achieving the happiness and fulfillment we are capable of achieving.

However, the acceptance of suffering is unnecessary; we all have within ourselves the key to creating positive life change. Once we uncover this key, we can master our fears and transform anxious, negative energy into an affirmative, life-changing force. In this chapter, you will learn which fears typically block the change process and how to eliminate them. You will define the changes you want to make and confirm your commitment to putting those changes into effect. And you will discover important inner resources that will enable you to transform your life. Such self-discovery enabled Margo Chevers to move off the welfare rolls and onto the stage of her own television show. Let us now turn to her story.

FROM WELFARE MOTHER TO TV PERSONALITY

Margo Chevers was born and raised in southern Massachusetts where she still lives. Her warm, outgoing personality is ideally suited to the public role she has chosen, her independence well matched to her entrepreneurial aspirations. A popular speaker and television personality, Chevers also owns a successful consulting firm. Over the past fifteen years, she has fundamentally changed herself and her life, moving from a position of seemingly hopeless dependency to one of confidence and self-control.

Like most women of her generation, Chevers was encouraged to marry young and depend on a man to take care of her. "This message was so strong," she noted, "that my parents didn't give me a middle name. Upon marrying, I would take my husband's name and his identity, and then my maiden name would become my middle name."

By the time she was twenty, Chevers had found a husband, but he was hardly the Prince Charming of her romantic dreams. Instead of the pastor or missionary expected by her strictly religious family, she fell in love with a wild young man who not only drank but also had a long history of trouble with the law. Not surprisingly, she did not live happily ever after, nor did her life follow the familiar plot of the fairy tale romance.

"A month after we were married," she explained, "he came home drunk and beat me. I should have left immediately, but I didn't. In fact, he beat me about once a week the whole time we were together. Our marriage was like a roller-coaster ride. He rarely worked, lasting no more than two weeks at any job. When he didn't have any money, he'd steal it out of my pocketbook. He was in and out of jail, and when I couldn't work, we'd be on welfare. We were always living under tension, waiting for the next bomb to explode."

When asked why she tolerated such a situation, Chevers replied, "I had no self-esteem, and he had even less than I did. I think that's why I felt comfortable with him. Somewhere deep inside, I also liked the excitement. I hate being bored, and living from crisis to crisis certainly wasn't boring. I didn't realize that I could get the same high by creating positive challenges in my life. And I was naive enough to think that when we got married we would become responsible adults. Marriage would supposedly fix everything. That in itself is a fairy tale. There was never any point in the six years we were together that we were responsible adults even after we had two children of our own."

Chevers hit bottom when her husband struck her as she was carrying her daughter. "I was terrified," she noted, "because I knew she could be killed. It finally dawned on me that the children were in danger, and so I decided to leave, but it wasn't really a grown-up decision. At twenty-six, I didn't know who I was, what I wanted, or how to treat myself. I denied my feelings and lived to please others. Inside, I was still a little girl, and I reacted to a bad situation by running away from it."

Within a year after leaving this marriage, Chevers married again hoping this time to find the prince of her dreams. "My second husband seemed to be the opposite of my first one," she explained. "He had a good job, bought me a beautiful home and car, and provided a good life for me and my children. He was, in fact, a liar and a cheat, a man who was as emotionally void as my first husband had been. However, he was a good provider and didn't threaten me physically. That gave me some security as well as helping me feel better about myself."

Chevers had moved from one dependent situation to another without stopping to look at her life. "My second husband just seemed to take charge," she continued. "A month after I met him, he moved into my apartment. Then he pressured me to get married, and soon I found myself agreeing. I still thought I needed a man to be happy, and I was very passive about making decisions. I still didn't know who I was or what I wanted.

"One day," she continued, "I was sitting on the porch

steps of my beautiful Victorian home, and I felt terrible. I thought to myself, 'I was miserable with my first husband, I'm miserable now. I have a lovely home, new car, plenty of money, what's wrong? If I get divorced again, what's going to happen?'

"All of a sudden out of the clear blue sky," she explained, "I realized that the one consistent thing through all my misery was myself. It was like a thunderbolt. I saw clearly that I couldn't blame anyone but myself for what had happened and that unless I stopped hiding behind excuses, my life would never change. I could say, 'Oh, my husband's a jerk, my mother made me go to church, my father never spoke to me,' but I knew the person responsible for my situation was me. That was the most liberating moment of my life! Suddenly I thought, 'I'm out of this jail. My life has been horrible, but if I'm the one responsible, then I can change it. I don't have to depend on anyone else to do it for me.'"

When Margo Chevers changed her attitude toward her situation, she took the first step toward changing her life. Once she realized that she was responsible for her own happiness, she experienced a tremendous sense of freedom. "I started asking lots of questions," she continued, "and I wanted the answers. I had done everything a woman was supposed to do, everything I thought I wanted to do, and I was still miserable. Why? Why should I feel this way? I was fully determined to find out."

UNDERSTANDING THE CHANGE PROCESS

For twelve years, Margo Chevers endured a life of unhappiness and discontent. Marriage did not bring the fulfillment she had been promised, and neither husband proved to be the hero of her dreams. She lived in a fantasy world that represented the negative side of the romantic ideal–passivity, dependency and misery–and accepted that fantasy as the only possible reality for her life. In short, Chevers adapted to her circumstances and grew resigned to her fate.

"I then hit the bottom of my unhappiness," she noted, "the place where I couldn't take it any more. When this happened, I told myself, 'It's got to be different. Life just has to be better than this.'" At that moment, Chevers took the first step in the change process. She confronted her situation, decided it was no longer acceptable, and acknowledged the possibility of something better. Taking this step is often difficult because somewhere deep inside we believe we deserve the unhappiness we have. Although low self-esteem does not necessarily lead to the violent misery Margo Chevers experienced, it can result in our adapting to a life of vague dissatisfaction, one that lacks joy, exhilaration and self-fulfillment.

Creating positive life change thus involves developing a strong sense of self-worth. For Chevers, this occurred when she was in a safe physical environment where her survival needs were adequately met. Another way we can develop greater self-esteem is to give ourselves approval, acceptance and appreciation. As we noted in the previous chapter, relying on ourselves for the three A's is the most effective way to increase our feelings of self-worth.

Although a strong sense of self-esteem is critical to the change process, the catalyst necessary for setting this process in motion is an equally strong sense of self-determination. For Margo Chevers, acquiring such feelings of self-control involved a fundamental change in attitude. During her first marriage, she regarded her husband as the villain, their marginal, roller-coaster life as his fault. If only he would stop drinking, stay out of jail, get a job, get them off welfare, then HER life would change. She was so caught up in blaming him that she was unable to see her role in perpetuating the situation. As a result, she felt powerless, unable to make choices, swept along on a wave of crisis and turmoil. Even when she left this disastrous marriage, she was reacting to the possibility of injury to her children rather than taking positive steps on her own behalf. In her own words, she was running away.

Chevers was able to take charge of her life only after she experienced a critical change in attitude. In looking back over her past, she realized that although she had changed husbands, changed homes and changed economic circumstances, her feelings had not changed. She was still unhappy and dissatisfied. At that point, she recognized that she alone was the common thread which unified all the events in her life, that she alone was responsible for what had happened. For Chevers, this was a liberating and exhilarating moment, a moment she experienced with joy and wonder.

DISCOVERING THE PRINCIPLE OF CHANGE

By looking at the same set of circumstances through a different lens, Margo Chevers found the key to creating positive life change. She learned that although she could not control people, events and circumstances, she could control her attitude and response to these things. She could choose to blame her husband, her parents, her religion or whatever else for her unhappiness, or she could take responsibility for her life and change it. In short, she had discovered what I call the "Principle of Change."

According to the "Principle of Change," we cannot control other people, unexpected events or external circumstances, but we can control our attitude and response toward these things. This principle provides the foundation for the entire change process. As Margo Chevers' attitude toward the people and circumstances around her became different, her life became different as well. In addition, by taking responsibility for her behavior, she experienced a tremendous sense of

25

freedom. If she, not other people, had brought the situation about, then she could certainly change it. No longer did she feel powerless and victimized; instead, she knew she alone directed her life. At that moment, she realized she could create something new and better for herself, and she was willing to face her fears in order to do so. By changing her attitude, Chevers was able to change her entire life.

THE PRINCIPLE OF CHANGE: PRACTICAL APPLICATION

The effectiveness of the "Principle of Change" was especially clear to me during a recent workshop I led for a large real estate company. The real estate market in New England has declined over the past two years, and this company felt the effects of that decline. Sales were down, employee morale was low and management was in a state of near chaos. I was called in to help alleviate the stress and soon discovered the source of immediate concern. A rival company had recently gone bankrupt, and the real estate broker and his staff were reacting with panic. "Since the competition can't survive," they believed, "we can't either. It's only a matter of time before we join them in the graveyard."

My first goal that morning was to change this belief. Until the company saw its prospects differently, it would indeed have trouble surviving. Helping the staff members view their circumstances differently was thus my first priority. No one had stopped to think that by losing a rival they could gain more clients. When I suggested this, the atmosphere in the room immediately changed. People began analyzing the territory served by their competitor and the number of potential clients residing there, and realized the potential for additional new business. They then computed the sales goals necessary to increase revenues to a healthier level and soon realized that reaching these goals was entirely possible.

26

As the individual agents began to see greater potential for earning, their enthusiasm returned, and they actually saw themselves generating new sales. Each person set higher goals for the next quarter, and each left the meeting feeling positive and energetic. Yet nothing external had changed; their rival was still gone, the market was still in decline. The change was in their attitude. Instead of seeing themselves helpless in the face of a disastrous economic trend, they realized they had some positive opportunities to increase their business. They not only saw the problem but also took responsibility for its solution.

RESISTANCE TO CHANGE

Sometimes we verbally express a desire, even an intent to change, but behaviorally we resist putting that change into effect. For whatever reason, we simply are unable to set out in a new direction. Resistance to change has three primary symptoms: procrastination, self-pity and the busy-bee syndrome. Let us examine each one in turn.

Procrastination

Procrastination means to postpone, defer or delay doing something. Its symptoms are clear: We simply talk about our goals without ever realizing them. Although it is prudent to think carefully before embarking on a new course, when weeks, months, even years pass without any action, then we are avoiding change rather than assessing the best means to put it into effect. Consider the following story.

Jim Vitello, a man who attended one of my seminars, wanted to start a general contracting business. He began gathering the information he needed to obtain a license, but a year later he still had not taken any of the steps necessary to get that license for himself. His excuses were endless--he needed to save more money, he had to pay one more year of college tuition for his son, he had an unexpectedly large tax bill. In reality, Vitello was not ready for entrepreneurship. He preferred remaining in a secure job to striking out on his own.

Procrastination is one of the most effective ways to avoid change. To conquer this tendency, break your goals down into small steps. Assign a deadline for achieving each step and write it on your calendar. Check each step off as you complete it. Remember, there is no perfect time to change your life. There will always be a reason to postpone change. The best way to initiate action is simply to stop talking and start doing. If you are unable to do this, then you need to look deeper at the possible fears that are standing in your way. We will discuss those fears later in this chapter.

Self-Pity

Another common symptom of resistance to change is self-pity. Feeling sorry for ourselves is an effective way to avoid making ourselves happy. We are so busy focusing on our self-pity that we miss all sorts of opportunities to bring happiness into our lives. This was clear in the case of Diana Jenkins, a woman who attended my "Who Am I, Where Am I Going?" workshop. At that time, Jenkins was almost fifty pounds overweight. Although she had tried many diet programs, she was unable to keep her weight down. "Special diets never work for me," she explained to our group. "I've tried everything, and I just can't lose weight. Other people have all the luck. One program or another works for them, but not for me. Being overweight is really a curse. I can't get a better job, my husband constantly picks at me, and even my children don't like the way I look. I'm fat, ugly and stuck in a deadend job. I don't know why things never seem to change."

Diana Jenkins was trapped in a well of self-pity and consequently saw her situation through a narrow and limiting

28

tunnel. She spent so much time feeling sorry for herself that she lost sight of her ability to change her situation. Until she dropped her "poor pitiful me" attitude, she could not drop her excess weight. Understanding and accepting the "Principle of Change" was a critical step for her to take.

If you find yourself trapped in a well of self-pity, allow yourself ten minutes a day to swim around in its dark waters. You must sit for ten full minutes and feel sorry for yourself out loud. At the end of ten minutes, how do you feel? How does your situation appear to you now? Now that you have wallowed--move on!

Busy Bee

The Busy Bee Syndrome is the third effective mechanism for avoiding change. For example, when David Hennessy, one of my seminar participants, did not get the promotion he expected, he decided to find another job. He made an appointment with an executive search firm and let his colleagues know that he was looking for a new position. However, within a month he had also initiated several other projects. Outgoing and athletic, he volunteered to coach his son's little league team that season. He decided to make his tennis game more competitive by running three miles a day and lifting weights. He joined a sailing club and involved his whole family in learning to sail–an exciting summer project. He even talked about remodeling the bathroom! Without realizing it, Hennessy had become a Busy Bee. Because he was involved in so many activities, he did not have time to update his resume or call for interviews. By avoiding his job search, he avoided the whole issue of losing the promotion and the hurt it had caused him.

If you are caught up in an endless round of unsatisfying activities, then you have probably fallen into the Busy Bee Syndrome. The best way to disengage from this syndrome is to withdraw from all but the most essential activities in your life. Stop everything even if this means doing nothing. David Hennessy was eventually forced to do this. He slipped during a ball game and broke his leg, thereby creating a three-month stretch when he was unable to do anything. During that period, he reexamined his career, faced his fears about changing jobs and made some important decisions about his life.

We engage in procrastination, self-pity and the Busy Bee Syndrome in order to avoid change. Even if we acknowledge our unhappiness and express the desire for a new life, we may still find it difficult to break out of our situation and create something different. Why is this so?

WHY CHANGE IS DIFFICULT

Creating positive life change demands that we sail away from the familiar into a sea of unknowns. It requires that we trust ourselves to navigate safely through uncharted waters. And it calls for faith–faith that whatever new world we discover will be better than the old one we chose to leave. The familiar is always more comforting than the unknown even if we are unhappy. Our unhappiness is, after all, ours. We are intimately acquainted with its parameters and demands, and therefore feel at home within its limitations. As a result, we often remain in unpleasant situations for years, accepting a shadow of the life we are capable of achieving rather than facing the challenges that changing worlds often generates. The story of Plato's cave-dwellers clearly illustrates this dilemma.

As you may remember, the people in Plato's story lived in a subterranean cave cut off from the world above. Their dark home was illuminated by firelight, their perception limited to shadows flickering on stony walls. When they first emerged from their cave into the sunlight, these people

30

reacted with apprehension and confusion. Where were the shadows? Why did their eyes hurt? And what were these strange, new objects all around them?

The cave-dwellers responded by fleeing this bright, new world and hurrying back to the comfort of their dim home. There, they took refuge among the familiar shadows, certain that they saw the world more clearly in the dark. They momentarily chose to live in obscurity rather than face the apprehension and confusion that moving into the light required. However, they soon pulled themselves out of the cave again. This time they remained steadfast in the presence of the sun, enduring temporary confusion in order to perceive the truth.

Gradually, the objects in the bright world around them became more familiar. Soon the cave-dwellers learned to rely on their own perception and trust their ability to see what was really there. Once this occurred, they never again wanted to return to the darkness of the cave. The joys of their new life were so great that they wondered how they had accepted the limitations of their previous situation for so long.

The experience of the cave-dwellers is a universal one. When we choose to change our circumstances, we often feel apprehension and confusion. Uncertain as to what we will encounter, we long to hurry back to our familiar world even if we were unhappy there. Effecting change requires us to confront our fear and hold fast to our chosen course. This certainly was true for Margo Chevers.

When asked how she felt upon starting a new life, Chevers replied, "I never dreamt what was ahead of me, and I was terrified. When I breathed, I breathed fear. What if I couldn't do it on my own? What made me think I could trust myself, take care of myself? I hadn't been able to do it before. Why did I think I could do it now? But that didn't stop me. Once I realized I had the power to change, I knew I could face my fears and keep going. I also knew that anything would be better than the life I was leading."

As Margo Chevers continued down the road to self-knowledge, she encountered three barriers that typically stand in the way: 1) fear of the unknown; 2) fear of criticism; and 3) fear of failure. We will now define these barriers and discuss how to overcome each one.

THE THREE BARRIERS TO CHANGE

Fear of the Unknown

Change means moving from one situation to another. It involves leaving something familiar for something yet untried. Because change involves facing the unknown, it is often accompanied by a wide range of conflicting emotions: excitement, anticipation, joy, anxiety and doubt.

When we embark on a new course, we cannot fully see the consequences of our decision or the exact transformation that the proposed change will bring. This uncertainty typically generates a series of pressing questions that we are unable to answer: What if we do not like our new choice? What if our problems become worse? What if our old life really was the best one? What if we cannot cope with the new situation or do not find the happiness we desire? Because we are entering unfamiliar territory, we are afraid simply because we do not know what will happen. Margo Chevers was explicit about this point.

"Part of my fear," she noted, "was that everything I did involved breaking new ground. I'd never seen any other woman go out on her own to find out who she is and what her life was all about. I wondered if my kids would turn out OK, if I would turn out OK, if my life would really get any better." Chevers ultimately transformed her life from one of dependency and dissatisfaction to one of joy and self-fulfillment. She did so only by confronting her fear and having the courage to keep going.

The following exercises will help you confront and handle your fear of the unknown.

Exercise 1.

Think about the change(s) you want to make and answer the following questions as specifically as you can. Write your answers or discuss them in detail with another person. Once expressed, our fears often become less threatening.

1. What is my worst fear, the worst thing that can happen?

2. Why is this so disastrous?

3. How likely is it to occur?

4. If it happens, how will I deal with it?

Exercise 2.

This exercise is especially helpful during those moments when you want to drop everything and run back to your familiar world. Think about your former situation and answer the following questions.

1. Was I happy with that situation?

2. Was it the best thing for my life?

3. Why did I choose to leave it?

4. Do I want to return to that situation?

Now repeat the following affirmation: I CHOOSE TO MAKE THIS CHANGE BECAUSE I WANT A BETTER (HAPPIER, MORE PRODUCTIVE, or any appropriate words) LIFE. THIS CHANGE IS THE BEST THING FOR ME RIGHT NOW.

Exercise 3.

Facing the unknown is as exhilarating an experience as it is a frightening one. When you set out on a new path, you create the possibility of new visions, higher achievements, greater self-knowledge and more contentment. Think about the changes you are making and answer these questions.

1. What is the best thing that could happen?

2. How will I feel when this occurs?

3. How will this affect my life?

4. What additional positive events will this lead to?

The information in Chapter Three, "Visualize Your Perfect Life," and Chapter Five, "Victory Over Fear," will also help you focus on the positive elements of the change process. Reading these chapters will further enable you to overcome your fear of the unknown.

Fear of Criticism

One of the strongest causes of resistance to change is the fear of criticism. We may want a different career, relationship or even hair color but are afraid others will criticize our choice. This fear is particularly strong when we lack confidence in our ability to choose what is best for our lives. Everyone who asks the question, "How can I make my life better?" has the answer to that question within. Nevertheless, very few of us look inward first and listen to our own voice. Fearing criticism, we shape our lives according to what we believe other people expect rather than according to what we want.

There are several reasons why people criticize us when we embark on a life change. They may be afraid that as we benefit from something new, they will lose something old. As they see us change, they may start looking at their own lives differently. This in turn will require them to face some of their fears and to leave the comfort of their familiar routines. Consequently, instead of seeing our transformation as an opportunity to reevaluate their own lives, they resort to criticism in an effort to abort our change and alleviate their discomfort. Because we anticipate such criticism, many of us avoid making any changes at all.

When asked about this issue, Margo Chevers was explicit in her reply. "It is very difficult to change against other people's judgment," she explained, "especially if they're close to you. After I left my second husband, I spent about two years exploring myself. I went out alone and with my friends, took classes that interested me, spent weekends away from home. During this period, I frequently left my children with my mother or with babysitters. The response from my family was awful. I could hear their loud whispers, see the criticism in their glances and body language. They simply didn't approve. This isn't how a mother was supposed to behave!"

In spite of her family's disapproval, Chevers continued on her course. "The times I spent with my kids," she noted, "were very exciting. They saw me laugh, and they saw me cry. I kept telling myself that the children were seeing a real person, a mother who wasn't perfect but who loved them a lot. I believe all of us benefitted from the experience. I grew and developed, and they learned that a mother has many facets to her life.

"I finally told myself," she continued, "'Well, who cares what people think! In the whole realm of things, what I do means absolutely nothing to them and their lives. If they want to talk about me, let them. It'll last for about one week, and then they'll be on to somebody else.' At that point, I felt confident enough in myself to know I was doing the right thing. Once I felt that way, other people's opinions became meaningless."

If fear of criticism is a problem for you, the following tips will help you confront and eliminate that fear.

1. Return to Chapter One and work on the Three A's. A strong sense of self-confidence and healthy self-esteem are the best antidotes to the fear of criticism. The more you trust and believe in yourself, the more easily you will create and effect positive change in your life.

2. Join a support group for people in your situation. Whether you are changing careers, starting a business, battling an addiction or getting a promotion, there is a support group to help with your particular transition. The YMCA/YWCA, professional and civic groups, and the library are all good sources of information. Check their publications and bulletin boards. Your pastor, physician, teacher and friends are also excellent resources. Once you begin looking, you will discover groups everywhere. If you do not, then try starting one.

3. Read self-help books and attend personal or career development seminars sponsored by your local adult education, community college or civic associations. A bibliography is included at the back of this book.

4. Review the "Principle of Change": You cannot change people, events and circumstances, but you can change your attitude toward these things. Margo Chevers initially worried about what others would think of her. However, as she gained confidence, she was able to change her attitude regarding this issue, and she slowly accepted that other people's opinions were unimportant. The important thing, she realized, was doing what was best for herself. Once she changed her attitude, her fear of criticism diminished, and she enthusiastically proceeded with her plans.

Fear of Failure

The final barrier to effecting positive change is fear of failure. Whenever we try something new, our first response frequently is, What if I really can't do this? What if I fail? Margo Chevers clearly remembers her fear when she suddenly found herself with a job after several years of not working outside the home.

"When I first was on my own," she explained, "I thought I would never get a job of any substance. I had no idea of my intelligence and capability, so going off welfare was a big decision for me. On January 1st, my goal was to get off welfare by the end of the year. Six months later, I had a job in a coffee shop and was financially independent. When I started out, I was scared to death. I look back now and am amazed. I actually thought I couldn't handle serving somebody a cup of coffee and getting them a doughnut."

When asked how she handled her fear, Chevers quickly replied, "I just took it one day at a time and didn't project too far into the future. I set small challenges for myself, met them and then set bigger ones. Over the years, I've learned to take my life step by step. You don't go from being on welfare to owning your own business all at once. Change is a gradual process. I moved from the coffee shop to a bigger restaurant to being dining room manager in a hotel. Eventually, I became sales director at a bigger hotel. Because I was successful at each job, my confidence grew, and I was able to move on to a more challenging position.

"There were two things that helped me move ahead," she continued, "The first was goal setting, and the second was the power of positive thinking. I managed an apartment complex, and associates of the owner would come in and talk to me. They were all in business and had been very successful. I'd look at them and ask myself, 'What makes them different from me? They're no more intelligent, have no more energy. Why are they so successful?'

"It finally dawned on me," she noted, "that it was their attitude. When they go to a bank and ask for a million dollars, they never once think they won't get it. In everything they do, they expect a positive outcome. It never occurs to them that something could go wrong. And if it does, they know they will rise to the occasion and deal with it. This was absolutely astounding to me. By thinking positively, they created something positive.

"If you truly believe in something," she concluded, "you'll find a way to do it because you're doing what you are supposed to be doing. You may have to go through trials and hardships, but they have lessons to teach you if you are willing to learn. I thank God I married my first husband. I'm thankful for my second marriage as well. Without these experiences, I'd be the same immature person I was. Now I know who I am, and this has brought me a deep internal sense of satisfaction. Nobody has been able to do for me what I've been able to do for myself. It is worth every risk I've taken, and every challenge I've set up and met."

You, like Margo Chevers, are capable of overcoming your fear of failure and meeting the challenge of positive life change. The following will help you break this final barrier.

1. Goal Setting.

Set manageable, realistic goals. Write them down and reread them often. Give yourself a deadline for meeting your goals and check your progress weekly and monthly. Chapter Four, "Ready, Get Set, Goals," will help you with goal setting.

2. Life Challenges.

Write down each life challenge you have already met. Answer the following questions:

a. What frightened me the most about meeting this challenge?

b. How realistic was this fear?

c. How did I handle this fear?

d. What enabled me to meet this challenge? List both skills and personal qualities.

e. How has my prior success led to greater success?

f. Now write a brief note of congratulations to yourself. Include compliments about your strengths and abilities.

3. Perceived Failures.

What, if anything, do you perceive as the worst failure of your life? How did you handle it? What was the outcome? How do you feel about it now? To what extent was it really a failure?

CONCLUSION

By thinking positively about the change process and its effect on your life, you will achieve positive results. The more you focus on your fear, the greater that fear will become; it will grow and thrive commensurate with the attention you give it. Instead of focusing on your negative emotions, concentrate on your goal instead. Think about the changes you want to make, the results you want to achieve and the exciting transformation you will experience. This will enable you to draw energy away from the negative and redirect it toward the positive, thereby increasing the possibility of success. In addition, work on visualizing a positive outcome and on setting measurable, realistic goals. (Turn to Chapters Three and Four for help in these areas.)

Remember, even for Plato's cave-dwellers, the process of growth and self-illumination was gradual. At first, they were most comfortable in a dark cave where they perceived shadows as true reality. After emerging from the cave, they had to grow accustomed to the light. Still unable to apprehend the full splendor of the objects around them, they concentrated on understanding reflections in the water. Finally, they were able to look upon the sun and see the world in all its true splendor.

Change is an ongoing process. It generates a continuing tension between positive and negative emotions, fear and the mastery of fear, challenge and the meeting of that challenge. Choosing to create positive life change means choosing to take responsibility for your life. It means discovering your own unique combination of desires, interests, strengths and abilities. And it means accepting each stage of the change process as you move from your own self-imposed darkness out into the sun.

Challenge To The Reader

Make a commitment to becoming all you are capable of becoming. Initiate positive change in your life today.

I accept this challenge.

_____   _____
Name   Date

Make A Commitment To Change

1. Areas of Present Dissatisfaction

   CAREER   FINANCIAL   PERSONAL   RELATIONSHIP

2. Possible Changes

   CAREER   FINANCIAL   PERSONAL   RELATIONSHIP

3. I want to change because_____

   _____

4. When I think about making this change, I feel (positive emotions)_____

   _____

5. When I think about making this change, I feel (negative emotions)_____

   _____

6. My specific fears are _____

   _____

7. I will overcome these fears by_____

   _____

CHAPTER THREE

VISUALIZE YOUR PERFECT LIFE

> *There is nothing either good or*   ✱
> *bad but thinking makes it so.*
> – Shakespeare, Hamlet, II, ii

Last year I attended a workshop in the beautiful desert of Sedona, Arizona. My purpose in going there was to sharpen my visualization skills, and the results far exceeded my expectations. What I achieved now seems as magical as the vast desert itself. The final session of the week-end program was, appropriately, held outside. When I stepped out onto the sun-filled patio, there before me were several mysterious, cloth-draped objects. These shrouded forms immediately raised my curiosity, and I was doubly puzzled when the group leader uncovered one near where I was standing. There, resting on two concrete blocks, was a pine board two inches thick. This was a seminar tool totally different from the usual flip charts, blackboards and overhead projectors I was accustomed to seeing.

What was the point of the exercise?

Later that afternoon, my question was answered. Thanks to these simple props, I was to experience once again the tremendous power of the mind. The assignment was to break the board without using, or even visualizing, force. At the outset, the group leader told us, "Imagine that the board is not there. You don't see it, you don't feel it, it's just not there. Visualize your hand moving through thin air, floating downward like a feather until it touches the ground. Your hand will move through this empty space with no effort at all."

The first volunteer completed the exercise without any problem. Then it was my turn to try. Remembering our leader's instructions, I closed my eyes and saw nothing but space between the concrete blocks. The board was not there. Slowly and gently I moved my hand downward through this empty space until I felt my fingers touch the ground. Right at that moment I heard something crash onto the floor, and I opened my eyes. There on the ground next to me were the broken pieces of board. I could hardly believe what I saw because I HADN'T FELT ANYTHING AT ALL. I had split the board in two with no physical force, only with the force of my thoughts. In my mind, I had removed the barrier, and in reality the barrier was no longer there.

The majority of the people in the workshop that day were unable to complete the exercise. "I tried to see the board disappear," said one. "The board was there, and I knew it," said another. "I tried to see my hand going through the board, but it just didn't work," a third noted. After listening to many such comments, I realized that although the group leader had given us the key, most of the participants were unable to use it to unlock their mental powers. In their mind, the barrier remained, and because they visualized the board, their hand encountered it.

THE POWER OF THE MIND

Visualization is the most powerful tool people have. It is the most important means to personal, career and business success, and we carry the only instrument we need to do it with us at all times. Visualization requires no special equipment, no employees, no outside assistance and no money, yet surprisingly few people avail themselves of this potent inner force. One reason for this is lack of confidence and self-acceptance. We often do not trust that we hold the best vision for ourselves within, that we know what is good for our own welfare. We do not trust our imagination, the inner voice that will guide us to the best choice for our individual lives. We also do not believe that having what we want is possible, that we deserve happiness, success, love, money or other good things in our lives. Consequently, most of us visualize either negative events or nothing at all. Then, when negative circumstances happen to us or, worse, nothing happens and our lives become stagnant and meaningless, we blame other people, our society, the economy, the schools, the government, our parents or anything else which comes to mind.

People who like and accept themselves are capable of envisioning positive things in their life. Moreover, they can see themselves achieving and accepting what they imagine. In contrast, people who are driven by self-doubt believe they cannot have what they want. Consequently, they visualize negative circumstances and then work feverishly to prevent the imagined disaster from happening. However, the more driven they are to fight what they visualize, the more likely it is that this very misfortune will occur. By directing their energies toward what they fear, they actually cause it to happen. The first step to breaking this negative cycle is meeting the challenge of self-acceptance. The next step is learning to visualize.

✦ Remember, your thoughts are the strongest influence on your life. They determine who you are, what you do and what you become. Learning to control your thoughts and visualize positive images is thus an essential part of creating positive life change. As Shakespeare noted almost four-hundred years ago, "There is nothing either good or bad, but thinking makes it so."

BARRIERS TO VISUALIZATION

When we decide to make a life-change, be it personal, career or business, a clear vision of the desired result is vital. Once we can envision something as possible, that something is ours. If we are unable to see it, we are unable to have it. Although we are all born with the capacity to visualize, there are certain barriers we create that prevent us from visualizing successfully. The five most common barriers are: 1) lack of practice; 2) negative self-messages; 3) improper framing; 4) lack of trust; 5) fear of fuzziness. Everyone encounters one or more of these barriers at some time. The following exercises will help you identify and overcome the barriers that are most problematic for you.

1. Lack of Practice

Many people are unable to visualize anything simply because they have never tried. In my seminars, I start by asking the group to visualize an apple, and a number of people usually react with discomfort. At that point, I ask, "Is anyone here unable to see the apple?" Inevitably, a number of hands go up, and people are relieved to discover that they are not unique. Visualization, like any other mental exercise, requires practice. It is impossible to envision a sweeping life change if you cannot see an apple. To sharpen your visualization skills, start with this simple process.

Set aside fifteen minutes during which you will not be

interrupted. Sit quietly, close your eyes and focus your attention on your breathing. Breathe deeply for one or two minutes. Now visualize an apple. The apple is round and green. Visualize the color changing from green to gold and then to red. The shape of the apple becomes oblong instead of round. Now envision the apple turning gold again.

How clearly are you able to see, feel, smell the apple? Keep practicing until you can almost taste the fruit. This exercise will help you develop the ability to produce mental images at will. If you find the process difficult, do not get discouraged. Try changing the object. You may find other things easier to envision. Above all, be persistent with your efforts.

2. Negative Self-Messages

When asked to imagine their perfect life, many people respond with the simple statement "I can't" followed by one of these reasons:

1. It is impossible for me to have what I want.

2. I don't have any choice right now.

3. I have to consider my _____
   (spouse, children, family, boss, co-workers, etc.) first.

4. I don't have the_____
   (time, money, ability, education, resources, etc.).

5. I couldn't have it anyhow.

6. It's wrong.

7. My _____
   (spouse, children, family, boss, etc.) expect(s)
   something different from me.

These negative messages surface from time to time for all of us. The key is to silence them as quickly as possible. Otherwise, they may become lodged in your mind, displacing more positive thoughts and distorting your vision of what is possible. The following exercise will help you eliminate negative thinking and enhance your ability to visualize your perfect life.

Step 1.

When negative thoughts arise, do not resist them. Respect whatever surfaces and accept it fully. Close your eyes and repeat the following: This is part of my thinking. I generated this thought and now I can eliminate it.

Step 2.

Create a place to discard your negative thoughts, and set them aside. One of my clients uses a Macintosh computer. On the lower right-hand corner of her monitor screen is a tiny trash can. When she no longer wants or needs a file, she simply drags the file name across the screen and puts it into the can. During our visualization exercises, she imagined that little trash can in one corner of her mind. When negative messages surfaced, she simply acknowledged them and then dragged them across her mental screen and dumped them into the trash.

Step 3.

Set aside fifteen minutes each day to do this exercise. Repeat the exercise until your negative messages are silenced.

3. Improper Framing

Sometimes we cannot generate a positive vision because we frame the picture we want incorrectly. It is possible to see the same situation in a variety of ways, to interpret the same set of data differently depending on the limits we impose. If we surround our lives with a narrow, rigid frame, then we severely limit the picture that can develop inside. The importance of proper framing and limit-free thinking became clear to me when I was a teacher.

Every year before school started, I was given the test scores achieved by my students. Although I was not initially aware of it, each test result became a frame or reference through which I saw that particular child. Those children with higher IQs were grouped together for reading and math, while those with lower scores became the "slow learners." As the year progressed, the different groups inevitably achieved the results that their test scores predicted.

One year, I decided that I was going to look at each child through a different frame. I had always believed that every person has an unlimited potential for learning, and I was tired of being unable to implement that philosophy more effectively in the classroom. Consequently, when I got the usual test scores at the beginning of September, I never looked at them. By discarding this limited frame, I knew I could give each child the greatest opportunity to expand, to be the best that he or she was capable of being. I also told the children that they had been specially selected for my class and that they were the best students in the school. This was not untrue, for each child HAD been assigned to me by the principal, and I believed that they WERE the best students ever.

The results were miraculous. The children told their parents and friends that they not only were the best students but that they had been individually chosen for my class. The parents in turn started expecting more from their sons and daughters, and also were more attentive to my communications. Almost no one missed a parent conference, and I received all the extra materials and support I needed for class projects.

I set up the curriculum differently as well. There were no reading groups. Instead, we had an open classroom, and the brightest children helped the slower ones without even realizing it. Excitement and achievement rippled through the classroom. Discipline problems decreased, the children were more creative, and everyone scored higher than grade level in reading and math at the end of the year.

I knew that something special had occurred when another teacher complained to the principal that I had been assigned all the high IQ children that year, and that she, therefore, was stuck with all the slow learners. In fact, what we achieved could be replicated in any classroom. It is a perfect example of limit-free thinking. By changing the frame that was usually placed around each child, I changed the picture that was developing inside.

Changing the frame you have constructed around your life may be necessary before you can complete your perfect life vision. For example, you dislike your job and want to make a career change. However, you need more training to compete for the job you want. You also have mortgage payments and a family to support. The picture you see before you is thus framed by impossibility. The frame prevents you from envisioning a new life situation and, therefore, from perceiving opportunities and avenues that might enable you to achieve the changes you want.

To overcome improper framing, try the following exercise. Set aside fifteen minutes and sit quietly where you will not be interrupted. Close your eyes and breathe deeply for a minute or two; focus your attention on your breathing. Now visualize the change you want to make as clearly and in as much detail as possible. Remember that your vision is like a painting in progress, and you can change the details at any time. As the picture becomes clearer, note any negative limits that interfere with its completion. Visualize these limits as a frame around your mental picture. Make the frame as concrete as possible, i.e., envision its size, color, texture, material, etc., and then pack your perceived limitations into it. When the frame is complete, simply remove it from around the picture. Sit with the frameless picture for a few moments and then answer the following questions. How is the picture changing? What new possibilities do you see? Stay with your vision as long as you can, avoiding all judgments and qualifications. This exercise will help you visualize new possibilities for your life without externally imposed limitations.

4. Troublesome Twins:
Lack of Trust/Lack of Acceptance

Lack of trust and lack of acceptance are twin barriers that often appear together. When we lack confidence, we doubt our ability to create and choose what is best for our lives. As a result, we look to others for the solutions to our problems. A parent, child or spouse; a colleague, friend or co-worker; our minister, our therapist, an expert in the field–we give these people responsibility for decisions that only we can make. Although advice and support are helpful, we are the best source of information about matters that directly affect our lives. Furthermore, we alone can decide whether we will allow ourselves a better life or not. Our family and friends may tell us we deserve the best; however, no amount of external pressure will enable us to accept positive change if we do not believe we are worthy of it. Instead, feelings of unworthiness will cause us to visualize what we think we can

51

have, not what we really want.

The following affirmation will help you overcome the "Troublesome Twins." Repeat this affirmation every morning when you get up, every evening before you go to bed and whenever you need encouragement.

I AM THE BEST SOURCE OF WISDOM FOR MYSELF. I HOLD THE ANSWERS WITHIN. I TRUST MYSELF TO GENERATE WHATEVER I NEED. I ALLOW MYSELF TO ACCEPT WHATEVER I DREAM.

5. Fear of Fuzziness

In our results-oriented society, we are uncomfortable with vagueness. We perceive uncertainty as the root of indecisiveness, and indecisiveness as leading to the inability to take action. Lack of action, we believe, generates lack of results, which in turn indicates that we are in some way inadequate. Consequently, we insist on objective, measurable goals, and we demand facts, figures and other concrete data as evidence that we are progressing toward the desired end. This belief system encourages decision-making at all costs without allowing for the confusion and lack of clarity that frequently precede major transitions. Bypassing this period of uncertainty often leads us to making forced, inappropriate decisions.

Management consultant Peter Drucker has spent many years studying this issue especially as it applies to the decision-making process in American business. Drucker notes that most corporate leaders are unwilling to endure a period of fuzziness in order to determine the problem to be solved or the decision to be made. They want immediate solutions even before they fully understand the issue at hand. Corporate managers are thus under pressure to generate concrete solutions without time for creative mental exploration. In short, they are encouraged to ignore feelings of doubt and hesitation and to produce immediate results.

Avoidance of uncertainty in favor of immediate results is prevalent at all levels of our society. Success in school, in business, even in our personal lives is measured by numbers: how high we score on a test, how much we earn, how many activities we schedule into our lives. There is little room in this system for "fuzziness." Consequently, it is of little surprise that many people have difficulty visualizing their perfect life. They expect to sit down and envision the end result at once and in detail. Should this fail to happen, they become uncomfortable and stop their visualization efforts.

If you want to visualize a life change, allow yourself time to determine what that change will be. Be prepared to encounter a period of vagueness and even confusion. The following steps will help you work through any uncertainty you feel.

1. Decide which area(s) of your life you want to change: personal, financial, career, business, relationships.

2. Set aside fifteen minutes of uninterrupted time. Close your eyes, breathe deeply for one or two minutes, focusing your attention on your breathing. Now allow yourself to dream about the changes you want to make. Concentrate on the quality and feeling that you want to experience. The details will come later.

3. Buy a set of felt-tip pens in many colors. Choose the colors to which you are most attracted and allow yourself to draw anything that comes into your mind. Imagine what shape, form and colors

best characterize your new life and draw them.
You may start out with random marks or simple
rainbows. This exercise is particularly helpful if
you are not yet ready to visualize a concrete, detailed
picture of what you want. It will help you define
the quality you want in your life, i.e., brightness,
motion, stability, complexity, simplicity, etc.

4. Close your eyes and visualize the patterns and
colors that you have drawn. What concrete pictures
start to emerge?

5. Keep a notebook and pen next to your bed. When
you first wake up in the morning, start writing. Don't
stop to think or correct your writing, just write.
Possible topics: What do I want my life to be?
What kind of person do I want to be? What kind
of work do I want to do? What qualities does my
ideal partner have?

6. Remember a time when you felt really happy and
successful. What was it about yourself and your life
that you liked? Visualize that quality and those
circumstances in your life now. What form do
they take?

7. Look for pictures that embody what you want in
your life. Cut them out and make a personal notebook
of images. Note any changes in the forms that
attract you.

MINDPOWER ON THE SLOPES

Once you learn how to visualize, you will quickly find
that your mental pictures exert a powerful influence on your

life. In fact, you will become and achieve exactly what you imagine. The story of Sam Reston, a participant in one of my motivational seminars, clearly illustrates this point. Sam is an insurance agent in his mid 30s. He is successful on the job, but his long-time fear of heights had prevented him from achieving success on the ski slopes. Athletic and in good physical shape, Sam wanted to learn how to ski but was afraid to face the lifts.

"I panicked at the thought of going up there on those little chairs," he told the group, "yet I knew if I wanted to learn to ski, I had to face my fear of heights. The lift wasn't my only problem. I also dreaded getting up on a steep slope and looking down . . . much less skiing down! Last winter, I went to the mountains with friends a few times, and one day I decided I simply was going to face my fear and ski. I got sick of waiting in the lodge while everyone else was out there having a great time in the snow."

Sam found visualization a powerful tool to help him overcome his fear. In his mind, he saw himself master every phase of the sport before he even bought his skis. First, he imagined the lessons and visualized himself as part of a beginners group. He then envisioned the entire group learning how to control their skis and make a proper turn. He heard the instructor give explicit instructions how to get on and off the lift, and saw himself following these instructions. He visualized himself going up on the chair enjoying the beautiful snow-covered scenery and then skiing down the gentle beginner slope one turn at a time.

"When the time came to take the lesson," Sam declared, "I simply did what I had visualized. We practiced the different turns and positions down near the lodge for about forty-five minutes, and then it was time to go up the slope. I was a little nervous, but went right along with everyone else. We lined up at the lift two by two, sat down and went up just as I had imagined. When I got off at the top, I could hardly believe how easy it had been. It didn't matter that this lift was very short and took about a minute to complete. The first time I did it, I really gave myself a pat on the back. If you're not scared of heights, it is hard to understand what a victory this was for me."

As Sam's skiing progressed, he realized that he would have to try higher lifts and steeper slopes in order to improve. The beginner slopes eventually were not challenging enough, and he became a little bored. "I knew if I wanted to get any better," he continued, "I would have to go right up there and ski down the mountain. That meant long lift rides and facing slopes that looked to me like sheer vertical drops. Every night before I went to bed, I imagined a steep mountain slope with a lift going up the side. I decided that this lift could let me off any place I wanted even if it was just a little way up the hill. Each night I saw myself going up a little further on the slope, getting off, and coming down turn by turn, my eyes fixed on a point at the bottom of the hill. It took me the better part of the winter to accomplish my goal, but I mastered that mountain in my mind pole by pole before I actually got out there and skied it. I may never be a daredevil on skiis, but I ski, and to me that is a major accomplishment."

BELIEVE AND ACHIEVE: VISUALIZING LIFE CHANGE

You, like Sam Reston, have the ability to create a positive life change. Visualizing what you want is a critical step in the change process. Remember, you can have whatever you can see. If you cannot envision something as real and true, you cannot bring it into your life. Visualization is simple but not necessarily easy. It often requires time and commitment. However, the more you practice, the more enjoyable the process will be, and the greater the rewards you will experience. As your ability to visualize increases, you will start to envision solutions automatically and naturally whenever you are faced with an important life decision. John Terravecchia, president of Cornerstone Bank in Nashua, New Hampshire, has relied on intuitive mental pictures to guide him throughout his long and successful career, often engaging in the process unconsciously. Having just completed a merger between his former institution, Derry Bank, and Cornerstone, Terravecchia fulfilled a vision he had first had for Derry Bank over twenty years ago. When asked how visualization has worked for him, he replied with the following story.

"I've always been very interested in geography," he explained, "and have a real feeling for where I am on the map. Most of the time, that map exists in my mind. If I am going on a trip somewhere in New Hampshire, I have a rough mental plan of the state, and I use it to guide me when I'm driving. I think I've applied the same principle to get where I've wanted to go in my life and to accomplish what I've wanted to accomplish.

"In 1969, when we first started the bank," he continued, "I visualized the state of New Hampshire and roughly projected the bank's growth. I took what I had read about population growth and change, and mentally put that on the map. Then I looked at the state road system and said to myself, 'If I were driving from point x to point y, which road would I use?' I tried not to worry about what the population was at a given point in time, but instead envisioned in which areas the traffic would flow.

"Hampstead was on a reasonably well travelled road at the time, and we decided to open a branch there. That was our first branch, and today it is our biggest. Twenty years ago, I had a vision for the bank that encompassed all of New Hampshire. In fact, I wanted to call it Bank of New Hampshire, but since we had already chosen another name, the board didn't want to wait the six months necessary to make the

57

changes. Even then, I saw us as something greater than a local community institution. Now the eleven branches of Derry Bank have merged with Cornerstone Bank, and we all have the same name. Cornerstone–it has a nice solid connotation and expresses more of what I envisioned for Derry Bank when we first started."

Some people, like John Terravecchia, are able to visualize almost unconsciously. They instinctively trust an inner mental process to guide them, combining factual information with an intuitive vision of the best course to follow. For others visualization is not, at the outset, an easy process. If you are such a person, do not be discouraged. Through practicing a few simple techniques, you will soon be able to envision not only new life goals but also the best path to achieve those goals. If you accept the challenge of visualization, you will soon change your life.

I accept this challenge.

_____   _____

Name   Date

The following tips will help you meet the challenge of visualization.

1. Set aside a regular time to practice visualizing even if you can do it only two or three times a week. You need at least fifteen minutes for each session. Make sure you will be uninterrupted. Start by breathing deeply for one or two minutes with your attention focused on your breath.

2. Ask yourself the following question: If my life (job, relationship, business, etc.) were perfect, what would it be like? Allow yourself to dream until a pictorial answer emerges. Be aware of the five barriers and review the appropriate exercises should one of these obstacles surface.

3. Imagine yourself doing what you really love to do. What do you look like? How do you walk, talk, dress? What do you do for work and for play? With whom do you associate?

4. What do you find most exhilarating? How can you incorporate this feeling into your personal life? Your work life?

5. Create your ideal image in the world of work. What are you doing? Where? With whom are you working? What kind of tasks are you doing?

6. How much money do you want to earn? What income do you see yourself generating? What income can you accept?

7. What is it like to do and be what you envision? How do you feel?

8. Check your negative images. What purpose do they serve in your life? What do they keep you from having? Why is this acceptable to you? Use the reframing exercise outlined above to discard negative limits. How do you feel once these limits are removed?

CHAPTER FOUR

ON YOUR MARK, GET SET, GOALS!

*To know that which lies before us in
daily life is the prime wisdom.*
– John Milton, Paradise Lost

April 18, 1988 – The day dawns cloudy and cool. It's a perfect day for running. More than a thousand contestants gather outside Boston ready to start the world's most grueling race. Boston Marathon XXI is about to begin. Its twenty-six mile course starts in Hopkinton, follows Route 135 through the western suburbs and joins Commonwealth Avenue in Newton. From there it is still 6 miles to the finish line at Copley Square in the heart of the city. Many runners start the race, but only the strongest finish.

It is noon, and the race will soon start. Among those lined up and ready to go is Jeanette Smith, an eighteen-year-old high school student from Millis, Massachusetts. After a year of rigorous training, Smith now stands with the world's top athletes waiting for the signal to start. Her lithe, muscular body carries the number 333, a blue band holds back her honey brown hair.

On your mark, get set, GO! The runners move out from the starting line, pacing themselves for the long course ahead. Two hours and twenty minutes later, Rosa Moto of Portugal crosses the finish line–the fastest woman in the race. At 6:50 p.m. Smith follows Moto's steps into Copley Square. Her time is nearly three times that of the women's champion, but her victory is nonetheless stunning.

Only three years before, Smith suffered a severe head injury that left her immobile, unable even to breathe. Doctors said she would never walk again much less run. However, this talented high-school track star had a dream, a dream so compelling that she could not give it up. In spite of physical trauma, emotional pain and a persistently negative medical prognosis, Jeanette Smith knew she would one day run the Boston Marathon. It was a dream she had had since childhood, and she was not about to let a head injury stand in her way. Through every week of her long rehabilitation to the moment she crossed Copley Square, Smith kept moving toward the finish line step by determined step. As it welcomed her with a cheer, the waiting crowd could only guess the effort that lay behind her achievement. Life had placed a seemingly insurmountable barrier across her path. What enabled this remarkable young woman to break that barrier in order to reach her goal?

On the following pages you will share Jeanette Smith's story. You will move with her from the intensive care unit of a suburban hospital to Lewis Bay Rehabilitation Center on Cape Cod and then back to the classroom–and the track–at Millis High School. As you experience her dramatic recovery, you will learn why goal setting is important, how to set concrete, measurable objectives and what personal qualities are necessary to transform your dreams into reality. Loving yourself, choosing to create positive change, visualizing your perfect life–these are the steps you have already taken. It is now time to actualize your vision by establishing and then achieving some specific goals. Jeanette Smith did just that and accomplished a miracle one lap at a time. You, too, can do the same.

TWO HOURS TO LIVE

May 25, 1985 – An ambulance stops next to the twisted piece of metal that once was a car. Four teenagers are extracted from the mangled wreck. One, a fifteen-year-old girl, is so severely injured that emergency workers fear she will die before reaching the hospital. Surprisingly, she survives the short ride to the emergency room, but doctors there give her two hours to live. Once again, she challenges their prognosis and continues breathing. Her family summons a priest to administer last rites, and family and friends join together outside her hospital room to pray. Two days, they now say, she may live two days. Her breathing continues. Two weeks, we'll give her two weeks. Hour by hour, day by day, Jeanette Smith pushes down the time barriers set before her.

THERE'S ALWAYS HOPE

Throughout those first, seemingly hopeless weeks, Jeanette Smith's family was always at her side. Dick Smith, Jeanette's father, is a strong, determined man whose positive attitude set the tone for his daughter's recovery. He never lost hope that his daughter would survive even when the doctors insisted otherwise. "We were told there was no hope," he remarked. "Jeanette would not live. If she did, she would never walk, talk or function out of a hospital setting. There was no hope whatsoever for anything different. My response to that was, 'There's ALWAYS hope.'" Goal-oriented right from the start, Smith immediately took steps to help his daughter recover. "We kept the radio on and played music all day," he continued. "We also talked to her and touched her. Whoever visited had to move Jeanette in some way, and she had constant stimulation eighteen hours a day. We kept trying and never gave up hope."

AWAKE AND AWARE

June 16, 1985 – Today is Father's Day, and Dick Smith is about to receive one of the greatest gifts of his life. Today his hope is rewarded. His daughter opens her eyes, the first sign that her coma may be ebbing. Emerging from a coma is a slow process, and the signs of progress are slight. Simple movements may or may not signify that the patient is regaining consciousness. Unwilling to raise false hopes, doctors therefore discount any movement they identify as reflex action and look instead for a "purposeful response." The definition of "purposeful response" proves to be a point of contention between the Smith family and their daughter's physicians.

"About a week after Jeanette opened her eyes," Dick explained, "we realized she could see. She also had some movement in one hand. So we began a new program with a new goal: purposeful response. I'd say, 'Jeanette, hug your mother,' and she'd reach up and give her mother a hug. I also made a series of Yes/No cards, and then I would ask her questions. The goal was for her to take the right card, that's all. We'd ask, 'Are you hungry?' and she'd take the No card.

"The doctors didn't acknowledge anything she did as a 'purposeful response.' They called it 'reflex action.' Then they'd say, 'Stick out your tongue,' and when she didn't respond, they told us she was still in a coma and there was no hope for any recovery. What would you do if some stranger came in and asked you to stick your tongue out? You probably wouldn't want to do it either. None of their attitudes made sense to me. Hugging her mother was not a purposeful response, but sticking out her tongue was."

63

After she had fully emerged from the coma, Jeanette Smith was moved to Lewis Bay Rehabilitation Center on Cape Cod. Although her doctor opposed the move, Dick Smith was insistent. He believed that with the right treatment his daughter would recover. He and his wife, Janet, visited Jeanette every weekend, providing love, encouragment and new goals for their daughter to reach. "We'd put coins on her tray," he explained, "and ask her to identify the nickels, dimes, quarters. We'd say, 'How much is thirteen cents?' and she'd pick out the right coins. Then we'd leave little cards with problems and instructions for her to work on during the week while we were gone. We'd say, 'Next weekend we'll do fifty cents.' That gave her something to think about and reach for.

"The staff at the hospital was wonderful, but they didn't believe in setting goals for a head-injured person. They told us such people cannot handle failure, so they shouldn't be set up to fail. Goal setting would do just that. Sometimes Jeanette failed to reach a goal, but that didn't matter. She just kept trying. They would reward any progress with a pat on the back, but the real reward for Jeanette was reaching a new goal."

In medical terms, Jeanette Smith had suffered extreme trauma to the brain stem. The injury left her in an infant state unable to control even the most basic bodily functions. Because her brain was so severely damaged, it no longer could send the signals necessary to direct her body and govern her mind. Even partial recovery from such injuries is very slow because the patient must relearn everything. Total recovery is rare. Consequently, the medical profession is reluctant to encourage head injury patients to set what could be defined as unrealistic goals. In an effort to help their patients avoid the pain and frustration of failure, medical workers often unwittingly guide them instead to a life of passivity and accommodation. Jeanette's indomitable spirit, her faith, her desire to run again and her committed family helped her overcome this syndrome and achieve what no doctor ever believed could be done.

I CAN AND I WILL

Although the doctors were wary, Jeanette Smith and her family had clear goals—the family that their daughter would live normally again, the daughter that she would run. Both were totally committed to doing whatever was necessary to achieve those goals. Both maintained an incredibly strong, positive attitude in spite of recurring despair. They all kept faith—in themselves, in one another, in God. For Jeanette, this inner strength helped her defy her doctors' prognosis and take her first steps around the track.

"My first weeks at Lewis Bay were terrible," she remembered. "They said I'd never be able to walk again, and that meant I'd never be able to run either. All I could think of was, 'I'm too young. I'm too young. I want to run the Boston Marathon. I want to do it. I'm too young to give up my dream.' Over and over I'd hear, 'You can't do this, you'll never do that. You're just wasting your energy.' I hate the words 'can't' and 'never.' I thought to myself, 'I can and I will.'

"My parents taught me if you say you can't, then you can't. They also helped me learn to be patient. Maybe you can't do something right now or maybe there's some good reason that it isn't possible, but you have to try. If you try and it doesn't work, then you can at least feel good about trying. Sometimes I got very discouraged, and then they would reassure me. 'You can do it,' they'd say, 'just give it more time.' I had no patience and wanted to do it all right now. 'Why isn't it happening right now?' I'd think. They would comfort me and say, 'You know you're going to do it sometime. Just keep trying.'

"Sometimes I'd get depressed, I'd think I couldn't take it any more, and I'd wonder, 'Why me? Why did this happen to me?' But I believe in God, I believe things happen for a reason. That's why I don't dwell on the negative. You always have a choice. A person who breaks his leg can say, 'OK, I broke my leg. What am I going to do today? Am I going to try to help my leg or what?' Fighting the injury doesn't help the leg, it just makes you a horrible person to be around. I don't want to waste energy dwelling on the negative."

As the months passed, Jeanette was allowed to leave the hospital for weekend excursions with her parents. Their first stop was always the track in nearby Yarmouth. While her doctors still believed she would never walk again, Jeanette was already dreaming of her first run. She soon felt strong enough to try. Her first effort was three steps down the track into her father's waiting arms. "After that," she remembered with a smile, "I worked up to ten steps, then twenty-five. When I was able to run one time around the track, that was the real starting point of my recovery."

HOME AGAIN, HOME AGAIN

April 28, 1986 – Jeanette Smith is released from Lewis Bay Rehabilitation Center. She walks away from the center, saying good-bye to the staff as she leaves. The neuropsychologist's prognosis now says nothing about walking or talking; however, he still is negative about her future. In spite of her miraculous progress, he believes Jeanette will be unable to drive a car, go to college, pursue a career. Only at Dick Smith's insistence does he omit the words "can't" and "never" from his final report.

When Jeanette arrives home, the reception is not what she expected. A head injury victim, she learns, is the object of suspicion and misunderstanding. Her high school principal is relectant to re-enroll her as a regular student, and many teachers are apprehensive about having her in their classes. "When prisoners get out of jail," she recalled, "people are suspicious and avoid them. That's how I felt, like a prisoner. People didn't understand my condition. They were afraid I wouldn't be able to control myself and would do something 'inappropriate' in class. Inappropriate–that is another word I grew to hate. People thought I would behave 'inappropriately,' so they avoided being with me. Before the accident, I had lots of friends. After I came home, I felt so alone. Every night I'd cry myself to sleep, dreading the next morning when I had to go to school.

"I started running again," she continued, "to stop feeling bad. Running gives me a high that I can't explain. I thought to myself, 'Instead of sitting home and feeling bad, I'll train for the marathon. That'll take up my time.' So every afternoon I went out running. That way I worked off all the problems I'd had during the day in school, and then I felt free, like I could run forever."

Throughout her long rehabilitation, she never gave up her dream of running the marathon. Now she felt ready. "I thought a lot about the race," she explained, "before I told anyone about my decision. For a couple of weeks I went back and forth in my mind, 'Do you want to do this or don't you? How will you manage training with school?' I knew it would be a major commitment. Once I decided to do it, I never had any doubt that I would succeed."

GOING THE DISTANCE STEP BY STEP

On the first day of training, Jeanette ran a quarter of a mile. "I thought I was going to die!" she laughed. "A couple of months later, I was doing only two miles a day and felt really discouraged. I wondered how I would ever make it to twenty-six. My physical therapist was wonderful and kept encouraging me. She would tell me, 'Run two miles today, four tomorrow, swim, bike, exercise every day, and rest one day a week.' Soon I was doing ten miles, then back to two, four, six. At the end of the year, I was running fifteen miles a day. They said if I could do thirteen, I could do the marathon.

"On the day of the race," she smiled, "I was really excited. I knew I could do it, but I was scared, too, and remember thinking, 'I don't want to do this. Please don't make me run.' I started out with everyone else, hoping that something good would come out of it. At the twenty-four mile mark, I wanted to stop. I thought, 'I don't want to do this any more. I'll be running all night, no one's around, what am I getting?' My brother was running along with me, and he wouldn't let me stop. When I got to Copley Square, I saw my parents. They were so happy! I heard the crowd cheering, and I knew I had done it.

"Running the Boston Marathon was my life dream," she concluded. "When I first started training, my desire was so strong, like WOW, I'll explode if I don't do this. You have to follow your dream before you lose it, before you lose this intense desire to make it come true. Then you have to stick with it and keep working to make it happen. You also need support. My family and friends were wonderful, and I had faith in myself, faith that I could accomplish what I set out to do. I'm proud of what I've done and happy that I lived my dream."

FROM VISUALIZATION TO GOAL SETTING

Jeanette Smith is an unusual young woman. The radiance of her smile belies the suffering she has experienced; her confident air masks the pain of each step forward. The obstacles she overcame could easily stop a person many years her senior, yet with faith, courage and determination she turned tragedy into victory over body and mind.

Throughout her long rehabilitation, she never lost sight of her vision. "They said I would never walk," she stated, "but I had this inner feeling that I would. I told no one, but I knew. My dream was to run the marathon, and even when I wasn't walking yet, something inside me said, 'You're going to do it.' I never stopped hearing that message."

Different people experience visualization through different senses. Some people see themselves accomplishing a certain goal; others actually feel their achievement bodily; still others, like Jeanette, hear an inner voice that inspires them to keep going. How you experience your vision is not important. What is important is to work until that vision is clear and compelling and then transform it into concrete goals. Why is this necessary?

A guiding vision is like the golden light of the sun. It illuminates our lives and fosters our growth and development. In contrast, a goal is similar to the rays of the sun going through a magnifying glass. The magnifying glass takes these diffuse rays, transforms them into burning heat and directs that heat toward a specific object. Similarly, goal setting involves transforming our desires and dreams into an urgent demand for physical expression. It helps us direct our energy toward a particular end. A vision is the overall guiding force, while goals are concrete, measurable achievements that help us actualize our vision.

Jeanette Smith's vision sustained her through trauma, injury and pain. As she began to recover, her desire to run only increased. However, she actualized her vision by setting new goals with each milestone she reached. By breaking the long distance into manageable steps, Jeanette reached the finish line one step at a time. With her family's help, she set and reached new objectives daily, weekly, monthly. Each success was measured in concrete terms: three steps, then ten, then twenty-five; two miles, then four, ten, fifteen; sitting, standing, walking, running. Breaking the twenty-six miles into realistic, measurable steps was an important part of the training process.

To actualize our visions and fulfill our dreams, it is necessary that we first clarify our goals and then establish concrete, measurable objectives. When we start visualizing, the images that appear are generally vague. Then, as we relax and trust the subconscious mind to guide us, clearer pictures begin to emerge. Certain images arise again and again, often with an increasingly compelling force. When this occurs, we are ready to define our goals and set our objectives. The following steps will guide you through the goal-setting process.

Clarify Your Goals

1. Write down the most significant images, pictures, sensations that arise during your visualization practice. Which ones feel the most pressing, the most demanding of your attention?

2. Pay careful attention to your feelings. They will direct you to what is most significant and appropriate for you. Remember, you must really want your goal or you will not achieve it.

3. Organize your goals under headings such as CAREER, FINANCIAL, RELATIONSHIP, PERSONAL. Invent headings if none of these is applicable. For example, under PERSONAL you could include PHYSICAL, MENTAL, SOCIAL or SPIRITUAL goals. Read over your goals from time to time.

4. Define your goals in clear, measurable terms. Ask yourself the following questions: How will I know when my

goal is achieved? What is the MEASURE of that achievement?

5. Set deadlines for starting and achieving each goal.

Check your progress regularly.

Summarize Your Goals

1. My career goals are _____

_____

One measurable objective is

_____

2. My financial goals are_____

_____

One measurable objective is

_____

3. My personal goals (physical, mental, spiritual) are

_____

_____

One measurable objective is

_____

4. My family/social goals are _____

_____

One measurable objective is

_____

BECOMING A WINNER

You, like Jeanette Smith, have a race to run. Although completing the Boston Marathon may not be your dream, you have your own finish line to cross. No matter what the distance you hope to cover, certain qualities will help you reach your goal. By cultivating what I call the Three C's you will easily pass each milestone along your course. With ✳ Clarity, Commitment and Confidence you, too, can actualize your vision and fulfill your dream.

The First C: Clarity

The fundamental requirement for successfully manifesting our goals is clarity–clarity of vision, of priorities, of mind. Why is such clarity important? First, without a clear vision of what we want, we will be unable to determine how to achieve it or to know when it is ours. To attain such clarity, we must go deep within ourselves and listen to our inner voice. When the appropriate goal emerges, we experience a flash of recognition, a feeling that says, 'This is it!' We then know with certainty that we are on the correct path.

Once our vision is clear, it is then important to establish our priorities. Sometimes we feel impelled to work toward several different goals simultaneously. At other times, one goal leads to another even before the first one has been achieved. As a result, we may fail to reach a single goal because we are unable to focus our energy in one direction. Instead, we try to move down several different paths at once,

72

thereby making little progress toward our desired end. Prioritizing our goals will help us avoid this pitfall.

To establish clear priorities, review your goals and order them according to the importance they hold in your life. Which one do you want to achieve first? Which one is a long-term goal? If you have more than two or three goals, keep working on the order in which you want to accomplish them. Remember that this order can, and perhaps will, change. Nothing you decide is irrevocable. It is the best decision only for the present moment.

Finally, it is important that you have a clear mind, that you are not blocked by negative emotions such as blame and resentment. Clarity of mind is one of Jeanette Smith's outstanding characteristics. Although she experienced severe emotional and physical trauma, Jeanette never blamed anyone for her suffering. She held no grudges and did not allow resentment to block her path. "A lot of bad things happen in life," she noted, "but you can't dwell on them. Sometimes I think about what I went through and get depressed. But then I think about all the good things I'm going to do. People who dwell on the negative irritate me more than anything. In the long run, life is much more positive than negative, but it's up to you to see and accept that. It's also up to you to realize that no one can do it for you. My parents supported me, but I had to run that race myself. I was the one who had to stop feeling bad and get out there and train and keep working toward my goal."

Blame and resentment interfere with our inner clarity and diminish our ability to achieve our goals. As long as we are controlled by such negative emotions, it is difficult for us to have what we want. The best way to overcome blame and resentment is to live by the "Principle of Change." Remember, we cannot control other people, external circumstances or unexpected events, but we can control our attitude toward these things. Certainly Jeanette Smith could not reverse what had happened to her. She had suffered a severe head injury, and her life was irrevocably changed. However, she could and did control her response to her situation. Instead of resorting to self-pity, she maintained a positive attitude and focused her attention on her goal.

The First Challenge:

Clarify your goal. See it clearly in all respects. Free yourself of all negative emotions that prevent you from reaching your goal.

I accept this challenge.

_____   _____

Name   Date

The Second C: Commitment

Jeanette Smith's commitment to her goal was another important ingredient of her success. At the outset, she wisely asked herself how she would handle the rigorous schedule, the physical and emotional demands of serious training. She understood that reaching her goal would require time, energy and hard work, not only physically but mentally as well. However, once she made the decision to compete, she faced the rigors of training without hesitation.

"Sometimes," she remembered with a laugh, "I would think to myself, 'What am I doing? I don't want to run all day and give up junk food. I want to sit down and rest and have a pizza and some ice-cream.'" However, she persevered. "Nearly half the runners who start the marathon," she continued, "don't finish. I often wonder how many more get discouraged and give up before they even finish training."

74

The most common reason we fail to reach our goals is lack of persistence. Unwilling or unable to commit the time, energy or resources, we simply give up. The only sure way not to cross the finish line is to leave the track. To maximize your chances of finishing the race, it is important that you understand what is involved in completing the course. Ask yourself: 1) How important is it for me to reach my goal? 2) How much time and energy will this require? 3) Realistically, how willing am I to commit my time and energy? 4) Do I have the necessary information to help me reach the objectives I have set? If not, what information do I need and how can I get it?

Although commitment is a critical factor in achieving our goals, flexibility is also important. Persistence does not mean forcing something that refuses to happen. No goal is set in stone, and sometimes more than one road leads to the same place. Successful realization of our goals depends on our willingness not only to commit our time and energy but also to change our approach whenever necessary.

In addition, a brief respite from the rigors of training is often necessary to renew our energy and sense of purpose. Commitment does not demand overwork. Jeanette's physical therapist wisely advised her young trainee to take one day a week to rest, to sleep, watch TV, eat what she wanted and relax. Taking time to rest and relax does not indicate lack of commitment nor do setbacks, slow progress or unanticipated change. You may experience periods when you cannot move as quickly as you expected, when the distance you cover is less than you hoped. The important point is to remain on course and keep moving forward.

The Second Challenge:

Work as hard as you can to realize your goals. Commit the necessary time, energy and resources. Don't give up when you encounter obstacles. Be flexible, but stay on the path.

I accept this challenge.

_____   _____
Name   Date

The Third C: Confidence

When we hear the word "confidence," we usually think of self-trust. Confidence, however, also means fearlessness, and the two meanings are obviously related. If we trust ourselves and our ability to get what we want, we then face our lives without fear.

Lack of confidence generates a negative cycle that prevents us from reaching our goals. First, we start doubting our ability to accomplish what we have set out to do. Self-doubt in turn increases fear. As our fear grows, it demands more of our attention. Then, instead of concentrating our energy on our goal we deflect it toward our fear. The more we feed our fear with attention, the greater it becomes and the more energy it requires. The result of this negative cycle is paralysis and subsequent failure to realize our dreams.

Real confidence is the courage to confront self-doubt and fear. It is the choice not to be controlled by these negative emotions but rather to focus our attention on our goal. When we are working on goal setting, it is important to continue building our confidence by reviewing the exercises in Chapter One. The more we have faith in our ability to succeed, the better we will be able to overcome our fear and focus on our goal.

This certainly was true for Jeanette Smith. In spite of her injury, she was confident of her ability to complete the

76

training even before she started. She believed she had the energy, determination and physical stamina to meet the challenge. Although she experienced moments of doubt and fear, she did not focus her attention on these negative emotions. Instead, she focused all her energy on her running and worked each week to achieve a new goal.

The Third Challenge:

Do not focus on your self-doubt and fear. Focus your attention on your goal instead.

I accept this challenge.

_____   _____

Name   Date

Evaluate Your Goal: A Checklist

MY MOST IMPORTANT SHORT-TERM GOAL IS

_____

MY MOST IMPORTANT LONG-TERM GOAL IS

_____

1. This goal is totally clear. I can visualize it in all respects.

2. I really want this goal. I am committed to achieving it.

3. This goal is realistic. I am capable of achieving it.

4. This goal is measurable. I will know when I have achieved it.

5. This goal is consistent with my value system.

6. I have the tools and information I need to achieve this goal.

7. My path of action is clear.

8. My priorities are clear.

9. My mind is clear of negative emotions.

10. I have complete faith that I will succeed.

CHAPTER FIVE

COUNT YOUR STRENGTHS

Enough work to do,
and strength enough to do the work.
— Rudyard Kipling

It is 6:30 Monday morning, and Frank Miller, the maintenance man at Cosmopolitan Insurance Company, is about to unlock the doors. He knows that Beth Burke, manager in the claims department, always arrives early on Mondays. Frank has worked at the company for sixteen years and is familiar with everyone's routine. At 6:52 Beth arrives, nods good-morning to Frank, hurries inside and quickly unpacks her briefcase. Today she must decide which of three candidates to hire as her assistant. By the time Tom Cotello, a claims adjustor, arrives forty-five minutes later, Beth has reviewed the three files on her desk and made a decision.

Around 7:40, Tom Cotello stops at the front door, coffee in hand, and starts talking with Frank. Friendly and outgoing, Tom spends ten or fifteen minutes chatting about the local baseball team, his son's Little League game and a recent memo about the company's possible relocation. Frank listens attentively and appears very concerned about the move. Tom hardly notices. He would welcome a change as long as he did not have to organize it.

Eventually, Tom moves on, stopping at Beth's door to continue his conversation. At 7:57 Eliza Schmidt, another adjustor, walks past. She looks knowingly at her watch and then at Tom before settling officiously at her desk. Eliza has also heard about the move, and she wonders who authorized the memo. Beth looks up impatiently, wishing Tom would stop talking and start working. She is just about to say something when he is distracted by the phone ringing at his desk.

Later that morning these four people join other company employees at a general meeting to discuss the move. As the personnel director talks about the future plans, Beth thinks to herself, "It's about time we moved to bigger quarters, I can't wait to get this over with." Frank Miller has a different reaction. He loves the old building where he has worked for so many years and dreads the upheaval that moving will require. Tom and Eliza are sitting together at the back of the room. "I hope they follow procedures in making this move," she whispers to him, while he wonders silently, "What procedures?"

Why do these four people react so differently to the same news? And how do their reactions affect their ability to work together and achieve specific goals? Researchers have spent years studying human behavior in an effort to answer these questions. The work of John G. Geier, a psychology professor at the University of Minnesota, is particularly important.

The results of Geier's studies show that human behavioral responses can be grouped into clearly identifiable patterns. Over the years, as people live, work and interact with one another, they develop a particular way of responding to different types of situations. Geier and other researchers found that these responses fall into four behavioral styles each with its own distinct characteristics. He called these styles Dominance, Influencing, Steadiness and Compliance (DISC). Geier eventually designed a self-administered and self-scored exercise, known as the Personal Profile System (PPS), to help people assess their behavior and understand the strengths and weaknesses of their ways of doing things. (DISC and the Personal Profile System are copyrighted by Carlson Learning Company. All rights reserved.)

Your approach to change, both at work and in your personal life, is shaped by the needs and responses of your particular style. Understanding the behavior patterns associated with your style will help you handle change more effectively and realize your goals with greater ease. In this chapter you will learn about your behavioral style and how to capitalize on its particular strengths. (For information about obtaining the Personal Profile System, write to CSA, 121 Allied Street, Manchester, NH 03109.) You will also learn about the styles of other people, to accept and appreciate those styles and to create an environment that will facilitate group harmony and productivity.

As you read the information presented here, remember that no one style is better or worse than any other. The strengths associated with each are necessary for any group to function successfully. Research shows that although everyone has a predominant behavioral style, the same person may exhibit characteristics of the other three styles under different circumstances or in different settings.

Now let us return to Cosmopolitan Insurance Company and its four employees. Ronda Markstein, the personnel director, called me to help the company prepare its employees for the eventual move. Ronda hoped to smooth the transition by helping people understand their roles in the proposed changes. To clarify potential problems, I started with the Personal Profiles. The results were useful and occasionally surprising. Each of the four people we met earlier conformed to a different style.

D–Dominance

Beth Burke, the manager at Cosmopolitan Life Insurance Company, conforms to the Dominance profile. People with a high Dominance, or "D", profile work hard to achieve results. Very action-oriented, they love a new challenge and thrive in an atmosphere of power and control. Their motto is "Do it now." Typical "D's" are competitive, with high ego strength, and, for these people, taking risks is simply part of life. Once a task is completed, they are on to the next one, eager to accomplish something new.

Beth Burke is a typical "D"–decisive, practical and assertive. In short, she moves quickly to get the job done. "I wasn't really surprised to learn I'm a 'D'," she laughed. "I know I'm fast-moving and a little impatient. Once I review all the information, I want to make a decision and then get the job done. I'd rather act quickly and take the consequences than sit around for weeks and finally let something happen by default. And although I want to see the facts before I decide, I'd just as soon let somebody else find them. Research isn't my strong point.

"I tend to be the same way at home," she continued. "It drives me crazy to go back and forth forever about which stove to buy or place to visit. On the other hand, my husband researches the pros and cons of every single thing. When we're planning a vacation, he reads every possible booklet on every tropical paradise and compares every detail. I suppose we make a good pair. He gets the information, we both read it, and I push a decision."

As she thought carefully about her behavior pattern, Beth

touched on an important issue: how different styles work together. Understanding that they approached tasks differently enabled her and her husband to work together more effectively and minimize potential conflicts. She also realized that, as a team, they were very effective. He was careful about details while she was more concerned about the "big picture"; he collected the facts and insisted that they study them; she insisted on a decision.

In addition, Beth recognized that, in the extreme, she could be impatient and that her behavior could be interpreted as domineering and pushy. However, she was aware that decisiveness was a characteristic necessary for the success of any group–family, business or community. She built on her strengths even while she understood their limitations.

I–INFLUENCING OF OTHERS

Unlike Beth Burke, who is predominantly task-oriented, Tom Cotello is more people-oriented. His behavioral style conforms to the influencing, or "I", pattern. Whereas Beth works on overcoming obstacles to accomplish results, Tom works to bring others together in order to achieve specific goals. People who follow this pattern are persuasive, spontaneous and accessible to others. Highly articulate, they generate enthusiasm for projects, thereby creating a motivational environment. The typical "I" sincerely desires to help others and is an eager, energetic group participant.

When Tom discovered he fell into the "I" category, he also laughed. "I was a little surprised," he noted, "but when I thought about myself honestly, I had to agree. I guess deep inside we all recognize ourselves when the right description is there. I enjoy working with people. That's one reason I like my job. Claims are stressful, and I can help clients with their problems at a time when they need support. I also appreciate the feedback when they are grateful I've done a good job.

That's where the recognition comes in, and, to be honest, I like it."

Outgoing and friendly, Tom likes interacting with people socially as well. High "I's" are often described as the life of the party. Animated and talkative, they enjoy being the center of attention and their motto could be "Let's have fun." However, in the extreme these people appear talkative and undisciplined. "I'm sure," Tom continued, "that Beth sometimes thinks I just go on and on. And maybe sometimes I do. But my positive energy is important to our group meetings. I think my enthusiasm and willingness to listen are really motivating for our whole unit."

Beth agreed. "Tom is great at generating ideas," she stated, "and he can be very persuasive. His desk may be a mess, and procedures aren't important to him at all, but he is really positive and energetic. His enthusiasm is very helpful, especially when there is a difficult project to be done."

Once again, Beth touched on the issue of working together to achieve common goals. Although she was more task-oriented, she recognized the importance of Tom's people skills. His approach was different from hers, but she realized that both were necessary to get the job done. As his supervisor, she was aware of his talkative tendencies, and she worked to help him manage his time better without stifling enthusiasm.

S–STEADINESS

People who conform to the Steadiness, or "S", profile are viewed as nice folks. Patient, loyal and dependable, they are the backbone of any organization and the mainstay of the family. High "S" people often have a negative self-image, believing their characteristics to be bland when compared to those of the other styles. However, others appreciate their calm reserve and good nature, and the high "S" is able to work effectively with everyone.

Frank Miller, Cosmopolitan's maintenance man, reacted to his Personality Profile with typical "S" aplomb. "That's me," he stated. "I'm friendly with everybody, but not too close to anybody. They know I'm there and they can depend on me to take care of things. I know everyone's habits, when they come and go, what needs to be done. I hate the thought of moving because everything will be different. I've been here a long time, and I like things just the way they are."

People who follow the "S" style emphasize cooperation with others in order to reach goals. Their motto is "Let's all work together," and they are adept at doing just that. When others become excited or upset, they exert a calming influence and work patiently until the job is done. High "S" people are good listeners, which contributes to their popularity. Careful and sincere, they respect tradition and like to follow the established order.

In the extreme, the steadfastness of the high "S" can appear as possessiveness, their desire for stability as insecurity, their respect for tradition as conformity. "S" people need time to process change. Once they understand what is expected, they shift gears and settle into a new routine. Tom Cotello understood this about Frank Miller. "I think it will be Frank," he noted, "who will establish order out of the chaos of our move. He will help us maintain some sense of tradition, of who we are as an organization." Without the support and care of such people, organizations like Cosmopolitan could not function nor could families survive.

C–COMPLIANCE (TO THEIR STANDARDS)

Eliza Schmidt, the other claims adjustor at Cosmopolitan Insurance Company, is a high "C." People who follow this style of behavior are accuracy specialists and are highly skilled at assembling and interpreting data. Precise, orderly and detail-oriented, their motto is "Let's follow the rules."

The high "C" is also a perfectionist who expects everyone to conform to his or her standards, to the procedures manual, to the rules.

Eliza was quick to agree with the assessment of her working style. "Being accurate is important to me," she noted. "I pay attention to the standards of this company and work to maintain them. I may be critical of other people's performance, but I'm just as critical of my own. I take the time to get the necessary facts so I won't make careless mistakes. Accuracy is critical in my job. I owe it to my clients to process their claims in an orderly, correct manner."

Like the high "D," high "C's" are task oriented, but they want all the facts before making a decision. Their goal is to promote quality in products or service thereby avoiding costly mistakes. Because of their methodical, fact-finding approach, their behavior is often interpreted as indecisive and overly cautious. However, their critical thinking skills and willingness to check even the most detailed projects for accuracy make them invaluable to any organization.

Although typical "C's" expect others to conform to their standards, they are nonetheless diplomatic in their dealings with people. Patient and reliable, they work well with those in positions of authority. High "C's" handle change best when given the opportunity to maintain standards thereby assuring that the quality of their work will not be affected.

THE FOUR STYLES: A SUMMARY

(Copyrighted by Carlson Learning System. All rights reserved. Used by permission)

Each style of the DISC profile has a clearly identifiable pattern. The chart below summarizes the typical characteristics of the four styles. Consider each style and circle the one that best describes you.

Dominant–Directive	Influencing–Interactive
F *Restless	*Emotional
A *Strong-Willed	*Enthusiastic
S *Decisive	*Optimistic
T *Efficient	*Persuasive
*Desires Change	*Sensitive
P *Competitive	*Talkative
A *Independent	*Open
C *Practical	*Stimulating
E *Daring	*Impulsive
D *Experimenting	*Charming

Compliant–Careful	Steadiness–Supportive
S *Perfectionist	*Dependable
L *Analytical	*Agreeable
O *Accurate	*Supportive
W *Persistent	*Accomodating
*Serious	*Predictable
P *Precise	*Calm
A *Orderly	*Patient
C *Cautious	*Modest
E *Curious	*Protective
D *Logical	*Sincere

Task Oriented <————> People Oriented

87

THE FOUR STYLES: NEEDS AND MOTIVATION

All of us filter events, information and the behavior of others through a private, invisible pair of glasses. The tint of the glasses is determined by the needs of our particular style, and we tend to distort or enhance what we see depending on the color of the glass. By filtering certain information in and other information out, our glasses often cause us to misinterpret other people's behavior. The employees at Cosmopolitan offer a good example of the process.

Beth Burke sees her company's proposed move as a challenge to be met as quickly and efficiently as possible. A practical person, she realizes the move will ultimately be positive for her and her staff, and she wants to complete it as soon as possible. A more methodical, cautious approach only makes her impatient. In contrast, Frank Miller feels threatened by Cosmopolitan's proposed changes. Since security, tradition and routine are all important to him, he responds to change slowly and with some resistance. Transitions are difficult for him to handle because he strives to maintain predictable conditions.

Eliza Schmidt also approaches change cautiously, but once she has carefully reviewed the facts and procedures, she then takes action in an orderly, step-by-step manner. During a period of transition, she will work to maintain standards even when conditions are uncertain. Ever optimistic, Tom Cotello handles change easily and without worry. The move is of little concern to him because he takes whatever happens in stride and follows the current downstream.

Beth Burke, Frank Miller, Tom Cotello and Eliza Schmidt all work together in the same company. Each has individual goals to achieve that, in turn, contribute to company goals. And all four must soon meet the challenge of an upcoming organizational change. Yet because their behavioral styles are so different, each needs a different environment to function

88

best. How effectively Cosmopolitan Insurance will move through its transitional phase depends on how well the needs of its employees are met.

What challenges Beth may only immobilize Eliza; Tom and Frank also will respond differently to the same set of circumstances. Understanding what motivates each style best is critical to maximizing individual achievement and reducing the potential for conflict, especially in periods of change. Given their predominant styles, what environment best motivates these four people? What best enables them to reach their goals?

High "D's" work well when allowed maximum freedom and the opportunity to achieve tangible results. Independent and strong willed, they need power and authority to make decisions necessary to get the job done. They respond well to personal challenges and continually seek new and more difficult problems to solve. Endless rules only frustrate these people, who thrive in a workable, unbureaucratic system.

High "D's" will respond best to you if you are brief and to the point. Unless they ask for lots of detail, such people become impatient when presented with too much information. They want to hear your recommendations and are satisfied when you take a position and state directly what you think. People with this style want to maintain control because they fear being taken advantage of. Lack of authority and loss of control are very threatening to them, and they will respond with resistance should they sense these conditions about to arise.

People who follow the influencing style are motivated by very different circumstances. Although they value freedom of expression, they work best in an atmosphere that allows them opportunity for public recognition for their achievements. Whereas the "D" is motivated by seeing the actual results, the "I" is motivated by the acclaim that this result produces. High "I's" flourish when allowed to use their considerable interpersonal skills and to participate in group activities. In contract to "D's," who tend to be individualistic loners, "I's" want the opportunity to share their ideas with other people and to generate group enthusiasm to get the job done. They tend to see a task less as an obstacle to be mastered than as a chance to enjoy the company and ideas of their colleagues.

High "I's" respond well to a positive, optimistic approach. Since they fear rejection and social disapproval, they work best when shown how their actions will gain recognition and favorable attention. They also want to keep up with new ideas and trends, and like tasks that provide them with an opportunity to meet this need. Highly creative, "I" people like the freedom to develop and express their ideas.

People who conform to the Steadiness profile work best in a predictable environment that allows them to establish a routine. They are motivated by sincere appreciation of their efforts and enjoy being supportive members of a team. Since they value stability and security, high "S" people dislike sudden change and are suspicious of unknown circumstances. Consequently, they need support, information and encouragement in order to move through transitions without resistance.

Strong group identification also motivates "S" people. They value being team members and need regular feedback regarding how their efforts contribute to a group project. The high "S" responds well to people who respect tradition and follow systematic procedures. They also like clear deadlines for goals and decisions. Unlike the high "D," who thrives on competition, the "S" works better in an atmosphere of cooperation and mutual support.

High "C" people like to work independently in a structured environment where they know and understand the rules.

When presenting new ideas to "C" people, have the facts at hand. If possible, show how your proposal will relate to or build on the status quo. List the pros and the cons and then provide alternatives. High "C's" respond best to a step-by-step process that allows them to absorb the facts before making a decision.

To be optimally effective, "C" people need precision work and the opportunity for careful planning before implementing projects. They respond well to others who delegate important tasks and then allow them the freedom to get the job done. Like the high "I," "C's" need reassurance and positive feedback about their work. They thrive in an atmosphere where standard operating procedures prevail.

Count Your Strengths

Understanding the four behavioral styles helps us understand different approaches to implementing goals and managing change. It also helps us understand why we approach a task in one way and our family, friends or associates approach it in another. Such understanding enables us to reduce conflict between people of different styles, to match people with complimentary styles, to provide optimum conditions for people with differing needs and to capitalize on the strengths of our own style.

Each category in the DISC profile has a range of characteristics. When assessing your own behavior or that of another person, it is important to consider two elements. First, any strength taken to its extreme can become a weakness. As I noted above, Tom Cotello's friendly, outgoing style sometimes results in too much talking. Similarly, in an effort to get the job done, Beth Burke occasionally pushes a little too hard and becomes a little too impatient. To maximize your achievements and enhance your relations with others, it is important to realize when your behavior moves from the positive into the negative range.

However, it is even more important to recognize and respect the strengths of each style without unconsciously distorting those strengths into weaknesses. We often look at our own behavior or that of another person and immediately find fault. "Jack's domineering and impatient," we say. "Sue's timid and insecure. I'm just a talker, not a doer. Lee is impossibly picky and critical."

In Chapter One, we learned that the first step to creating change in our lives and achieving new goals is to build confidence and self-esteem. We can do this best by accepting our strengths while respecting those of other people. Feeling either superior or inferior only reflects a lack of confidence and can create serious communication problems. Instead of seeing a given situation for what it is, we interpret another's behavior based on our personal insecurities. This causes us to distort what is there and then to respond to that distortion.

For example, let us imagine a possible response to Frank Miller's hesitation about his company's proposed move. A high "S," Frank is concerned with tradition and stability and shows resistance to the upcoming change. Without understanding Frank's need for security, Beth responds as follows: "I have to be tough with Frank or I'll never get him to cooperate. He's so wishy-washy and scared of the slightest change in his routine. This calls for immediate action on my part." How do you think Frank will respond?

When threatened in this manner, he simply resists and refuses to cooperate. Beth soon feels the situation slipping beyond her control, and she reacts to Frank with even more impatience thereby setting a negative cycle in motion. The more she pushes the harder he resists. This cycle is based on Beth's unawareness of Frank's style and her own. Instead of seeking him as a person who, with encouragement and support, can help her make the transition, she sees an obstacle standing in her way. A high "D," her reaction is to overcome that obstacle as quickly as possible in order to achieve her goal. As a result, her job becomes more difficult, and she is unable to use Frank's strengths to make the transition easier.

We can avoid this damaging cycle in our interaction with others by accepting and respecting the strengths of people with differing styles. However, sometimes this is difficult to do. The following exercise will help you understand why. The chart on page 87 analyzes the positive qualities, or strengths, associated with each style. Take a moment and review the four groups of characteristics. Now study the chart on page 94, which presents each style in a negative light. Compare this negative analysis to the positive one on page 87 and think about the following questions.

1. Why do you think you sometimes see other people's strengths as weaknesses?

2. What problems do your distortions cause?

3. How often do you react critically to a style different from your own?

4. What can you do to change your attitude and response?

STRENGTHS INTO WEAKNESS

(Copyrighted by Carlson Learning Systems. All rights reserved. Used by permission)

D–Domineering

*Pushy
*Impatient
*Tough
*Harsh
*Attacking
*Hasty

Fears Loss Of Control

—>Helplessness

C–Critical

*Picky
*Stuffy
*Judgmental
*Indecisive
*Rigid
*Suspicious

Fears Loss Of Standards

—>Chaos

I–Impulsive

*Disorganized
*Undisciplined
*Manipulative
*Excitable
*Reactive
*Vain

Fears Loss Of Approval

—>Rejection

S–Stiff

*Naive
*Insecure
*Awkward
*Wish-Washy
*Possessive
*Conforming

Fears Loss Of Security

—>Criticism

DISC–SELF ANALYSIS

(Copyrighted by Carlson Learning System. All rights reserved. Used by permission.)

The following exercises will help you understand your strengths as well as accept the strengths of others. Answer based on what you have learned in this chapter.

THESE ARE INSIGHTS I HAVE ABOUT MYSELF:

1. I recognize and accept that I have these strengths_____

   _____

2. I plan to use these strengths to _____

   _____

3. Other insights about myself are _____

   _____

THESE ARE INSIGHTS I HAVE ABOUT OTHERS

1. I recognize and accept that others have these strengths:

   "D" _____

   "I" _____

   "S" _____

   "C" _____

2. I can benefit from the strengths of others by _____

_____

3. Some new insights I have about others are _____

_____

The Challenge Of Self-Acceptance

Accepting the strengths associated with your style will help you build confidence. Greater confidence will in turn enable you to achieve your goals. Achieving your goals will complete this positive cycle and encourage you to reach for yet another dream.

I accept this challenge.

_____   _____
Name   Date

CHAPTER SIX

VICTORY OVER FEAR

Courage is resistance to fear,
mastery of fear–not absence of fear.
– Mark Twain

It was a bright, sunny day in May. I was sitting in a small plane high above the ground, my eyes fixed on the landscape 8000 feet below. The fields were brilliant green dusted with gold, the trees soft with new leaves. A second later the plane door slid open, and I heard my instructor's voice: "Sit on the edge, feet out the door, hands on your stomach." I looked down again, momentarily paralyzed by fear, and then moved toward the opening in the side of the plane. Suddenly I was free floating through the air toward the ground. I could hardly believe it was me! For a thousand feet, I floated freely, quietly, and then the parachute puffed open. There was utter silence. My ego disappeared. I was one with the universe.

I decided to go skydiving because I wanted to overcome a personal barrier: the need to control. In the past, I associated control with power and power with the ability to direct my own life. Unless I controlled my environment, I believed it would control me. As a result, I spent precious energy struggling to keep people and events from taking over my life. Over the years, I learned that control makes us feel as if we have power, but it does not empower us. On the contrary, the need to control causes us to react to our external circumstances instead of acting in our own behalf. When control is our goal, we forget that we have choices and blame others for our situation.

To face this issue, I chose a course called "Tandem Skydiving," and it took less than a morning to complete. The instructor and I went up in a plane, and within half an hour we were floating through the air joined together by a harness. On the way down, he supplied immediate on-the-job training, showing me how to land and how to control the direction of our fall. I could guide us to our landing site by moving the parachute to the right or the left. Whether we arrived on target was dependent on me; however, whether we survived the fall was dependent on my instructor. The parachute was attached to his back, and I was literally hanging in the air, connected to him by two metal clamps. As I floated toward the ground, I kept thinking, "I'm doing it, I'm really doing it." At that moment, I faced my fear, abandoned control and changed my self-perception forever.

When people hear this story, they always ask, "How could you take such a risk? You could have died!" To most of us, taking a risk means exposing ourselves to danger, and our reaction is therefore negative. The Chinese symbol for risk better captures the true nature of risk-taking than does our Western definition. It is comprised of two characters, one for opportunity, the other for danger and suggests that a seemingly perilous course can lead to a positive outcome. Skydiving certainly involves some danger, but once I understood the process, the danger seemed minimal. Assessing the risk was therefore the first step I took before making a final commitment to jump.

In Chapter Four, you set your objectives and made a commitment to achieve your goals. When you did this, you decided to jump from your own personal plane. You chose to move into unfamiliar space in order to accomplish your dream. However, you cannot make the leap without taking some risks. This chapter will help you assess and minimize those risks.

The first step is to examine your view of yourself as a risk taker. How do you feel about your ability to take risks and how does this self-perception affect your capacity for risk? Then, you will assess your situation and determine how much of a gamble achieving your goal actually requires. Finally, you will identify the internal barriers that most commonly keep people from taking risks. What attitudes prevent you from reaching your goals and how can you overcome those attitudes?

YOUR CAPACITY FOR RISK

During my seminars, I often share my skydiving story. People invariably respond by saying, "I could never do that. I'm not a risk-taker." However, as the seminar progresses, I am astonished by the varied and challenging experiences these same people have had. After casually dismissing themselves as lacking courage, they then describe accomplishments that involved tremendous risks. They simply did not give themselves credit for what they had done.

Every one of you has faced personal challenges successfully. You do not have to go skydiving to take a risk. Changing jobs, having a baby, purchasing a home–all involve risk, yet few of us would identify them as "risky." We respond instead by saying, "That's not a risk. Everyone does it." Such comments only undermine our confidence and reduce our ability to undertake new challenges.

One way to increase your capacity for risk is to give yourself credit for what you have already achieved. The following exercise will help you do this. Complete each sentence as accurately and fairly as you can. Be careful not to compare yourself to other people.

Step One – Your Capacity For Risk

1. One risk I have taken is_____

_____

2. I took this risk because _____

_____

3. The outcome was_____

_____

4. I feel _____ about this outcome

because_____

5. I handled this risk successfully because_____

_____

Whenever you doubt your ability to take risks, do this exercise again. Then repeat the following affirmation: I AM CAPABLE OF HANDLING WHATEVER RISKS I UNDERTAKE. I MEET NEW CHALLENGES WITH STRENGTH AND DETERMINATION.

DIFFERENT STYLES, DIFFERENT ATTITUDES

In the previous chapter, you learned about the four behavioral styles. The four people you met all view change, and therefore risk, differently. Their attitudes in turn affect their behavior. Recognizing how people with your style perceive risk will help you understand your own approach to risk-taking.

People like Beth Burke, who fall into the Dominance category, are action-oriented and make decisions quickly. As a result, they are likely to spend minimal time on the risk-assessment process. Although concerned about facts and figures, after considering the appropriate information, they take immediate steps to reach their goals. People with a high Influencing profile, like Frank Cotello, have a relaxed attitude toward change. Unusually optimistic, high "I's" often bypass a lengthy or formal risk analysis. Instead, they ease into a course of action with little prior planning.

In contrast, people with a Supportive or Compliant style are very cautious in their approach to risk. The high "S" is slow to change and finds it difficult to take risks even to achieve a strongly desired goal. The high "C" spends considerable time researching facts and figures to minimize potential risks. People like Eliza Schmidt want to assess the situation from as many angles as possible before taking action.

As you read the following section, keep your style in mind. If you conform to the "D" or "I" profile, you may want to spend a little more time analyzing the risks involved in achieving your goals. If you are a high "S" or "C," remember your tendency toward caution. Consider setting a limit on the amount of time you will spend collecting and analyzing information. The following section will help people of all four styles move through the assessment process as productively and efficiently as possible.

ASSESS THE RISK FACTORS

When I announced to my family that I was going skydiving, they were terrified. My husband was sure I would break a leg, and my children were concerned for my survival. Inside, I was also a little frightened, but my excitement was greater than my fear. Before making my final decision, I carefully assessed the danger involved. I would be connected to my instructor by strong metal clamps. The cords on the parachute were of durable nylon, and he would wear a second parachute in case the first one failed to open. He had many years of experience and had completed thousands of jumps without injury. In addition, his wife had photos of other people skydiving. Their expressions showed exhilaration, amazement, satisfaction.

After I decided to proceed, I had to sign three release forms, a reminder that there was indeed some risk. However, once I had the facts necessary to make an informed decision, my fear diminished. I knew the safety nets were all in place, and the risk now seemed small compared to the benefits I would gain. Here was an opportunity to increase my confidence, master my fear and reach a new personal goal.

When we want to create change in our lives and reach for new goals, we often react with anxiety. "What about the risks?" we ask ourselves. "How will I face the risks involved?" I do not recommend embarking on any new course without assessing your situation first. Facts and figures will help you understand exactly how much of a gamble you are about to take and whether the outcome is worth the risk. Once you have made such an assessment, you can make a better decision about what you want to do.

The following exercise will help you assess the risks involved in working toward your goal.

Step Two – Assess Your Goal

MY GOAL:_____

_____

1. In working toward this goal:

   a. What factors am I sure about?

   b. About what am I most uncertain?

   c. What factors are beyond my control?

2. What can I lose by working toward this goal?

3. What will I gain from achieving this goal?

4. How much risk is actually involved?

5. To what extent do the benefits outweigh the risks?

6. How do I feel about my goal now?

After completing this exercise, take a few moments to relax and think about your goal. Sit comfortably, close your eyes and visualize the desired outcome in as much detail as possible. See and feel yourself achieving your dream. When the picture is complete, ask yourself: How do I feel? What is my life like?

FINDING THE COURAGE WITHIN

During my goal-setting seminars, I frequently hear the following comment: "We've set our goals and assessed the risks, but now we feel stalled. Why aren't we making more progress? What's standing in our way?" Achieving new goals means experiencing change–change in our lives, in our relationships and in ourselves. Although we may genuinely want to reach the objectives we have set, we simultaneously fear the changes this will require. These fears then arise as inner barriers that prevent us from taking action.

Mark Twain noted that courage is not the absence of fear but the willingness to confront it. Most fears associated with change are generated by a simple lack of faith. We do not believe that we can and will achieve what is best for our lives. As we work toward new goals, a nagging voice inside us keeps questioning: "What if I don't make it? What if I don't like it once I have it? What if I lose something I love to get it? What if I lose control over my life?" All of us are born with the courage we need to silence these messages and eliminate "what if" from our lives. Let us now turn to the story of Roland Pelletier, a recovering alcoholic who faced his worst fear in order to stop drinking.

JUST AN AVERAGE GUY

His vital statistics declare Roland Pelletier an average person. At five foot nine and one-hundred and sixty pounds, he is of average height and weight. He has medium brown hair, medium blue eyes and is of medium build. Roland once described himself as "an everyday guy–average looking, average communication, average fun."

In spite of this self-description, Roland Pelletier is hardly average. When he was thirty, he found the courage to face his worst fear–giving up control over the world around him and facing that world without alcohol. Thanks to his inner strength, his intelligence, spirit and heart, he successfully met this challenge. "The day I stopped drinking," he noted, "I stopped trying to control everything. I surrendered myself to a higher power and gave the world back to Him to run. I realized that the only thing I had to learn to control is myself."

From the time he was seventeen, alcohol had stood between him and his fears. It had also almost destroyed him—physically, mentally and spiritually. "Alcohol," he remembered, "eventually became more important than anything else in my life—than my work, my family, even my health. When I stopped drinking, the biggest risk was giving up the best friend I thought I ever had, the source of my confidence and success. I used to be very shy, insecure and self-conscious. I used alcohol to avoid these awful feelings and to allow myself to take risks.

"I joined the Marines when I was seventeen," he continued, "to escape my father's constant abuse and criticism. I probably chose the Marines because the guys looked great in their dress blues. I was in desperate need of getting attention and approval, and I'm sure I thought people would admire me in my uniform. After basic training, I started going to a nightclub at a nearby naval base with the other guys. I loved the lights, the colors, the beautiful women, yet I actually felt bad inside because I couldn't participate. I saw other guys flirting and dancing, but I had tremendous fears of letting myself go and socializing with people. I wanted to dance but was too shy and afraid to ask anybody.

"One night this officer candidate who I admired came in, and I told him I wanted a drink that would make me feel really sociable but classy, too. I was sick of drinking beer. He said to me, 'The drink for you is my drink, Chivas Regal.' So I ordered Chivas Regal, 'on the rocks, no water.' By the third drink I was feeling very comfortable, and I went up to this beautiful woman sitting at his table and said, 'Do you want to dance,' and when she said yes, I almost said, 'You do?' She said, 'I've been watching you and wondering when you were going to ask me.' Right then I connected drinking with being accepted and part of a group."

Roland's goal was to excel socially, to stand out in a group, to be accepted and admired. "I thought I was building confidence," he explained, "because drinking allowed me to be funny and sociable. My fears just evaporated. I felt like I was breaking social barriers that had always stood in my way, but my confidence was based entirely on alcohol. Liquor allowed me to erase my insecurity very fast.

"I wanted to love everybody,' he continued, "and I wanted everybody to love me, so I started buying people drinks. I quickly learned this made instant friends. Partying at night gave me a chance to prove again and again how popular and successful I was. At first, I only went out on Fridays and Saturdays. Then I added a Wednesday, then a Tuesday. I started getting up in the morning with a few cobwebs in my head, but it was worth it. Soon drinking and partying became more important to me than anything, even the Marine Corps."

During this time, Roland developed an "I don't care" attitude that resulted in an undesirable discharge from the Marines. "I thought I knew it all," he stated, "and couldn't see what I was doing to my life. When I partied on weekends, I thought to myself, 'Who cares? If I get tossed out, I'll move on and make something else work.'" Thanks to his exceptional intelligence and capability, Roland did move on and, temporarily, did make something else work. After his discharge he found a job in a sheet metal factory, and within eight months he learned to read blueprints and operate all the machinery in the plant. In spite of his success, Roland's insecurity continued to grow and he turned once again to the most easily available remedy.

"After I experienced success on the job," he explained, "I decided to reward myself with a little more drinking and partying. I started coming in a little late and doing the work a little slower. This started a pattern that continued for years. I would go into a new job and see it as a new conquest. I'd

106

learn quickly, show I had talent and ability, and then reward myself with drinking. I went through seven jobs in four years. Each time the drinking started to interfere with my performance, I'd quit before they could fire me."

During this period, Roland began taking classes at the University of Lowell. Because he wanted to attend school full-time, he decided to sell vacuum cleaners at night, thereby freeing his days for classes. Once again he enjoyed immediate success. "Within three weeks," he remembered, "I was breaking their sales records and clearing $700 a week. I supported myself this way until I finished school. I was the only person in my family to go to college, and I graduated in the top ten percent of my class."

After graduation, Roland's career continued to expand. However, his inner growth did not match his external success. "I was very arrogant when the recruiters came to campus," he stated. "One man offered me over $14,000, $2500 more than he offered anyone else. I'll never forget it or my attitude. I told him I was already making $30,000 selling vacuum cleaners, and he was crazy if he thought I'd take $14,000 to push a pencil. I didn't even give him the respect of thanking him for his offer. So now I had an ego problem and a money problem as well as an alcohol problem."

Roland's success continued in spite of his drinking. Soon he was earning over $100,000 a year, but as his salary grew, his self-esteem continued to shrink. "I had learned to make money," he recalled, "but I spent it as fast as I got it on designer clothes, fancy jewelry, big cars. I had a tremendous sense of false confidence. It was a buy-your-way world, and I was very good at buying. Instead of saving my money, I spent three or four-hundred dollars a week partying, taking people out to expensive dinners and buying everyone drinks. I was very successful, yet felt as if I had to accomplish more and more."

Roland Pelletier was not quite thirty when he was forced to acknowledge that he had a serious problem. "I started having blackouts," he recalled, "my kidneys weren't functioning and I wet the bed. I also was terrified that I was going insane. I was getting sicker and sicker, but I was too scared to stop drinking. I thought without alcohol I wouldn't survive.

"One day I looked in the mirror, and I didn't like what I saw. Flashes of my life went before me. I saw a wonderful young boy who had had his first job at twelve and then I saw myself as I was: a drunken wreck. I remembered hating my father, feeling cheated, going into the service, feeling cheated, graduating from college and being tremendously successful at work, feeling cheated and feeling sorry for myself. For the first time, life was looking back at me from the mirror, and I knew the answer was there inside me.

"Soon after that, I was at my sister's. My niece, also my godchild, came up to me and I said, 'Give me a kiss goodnight.' She said, 'I don't want to because you act funny and you smell funny.' That hit me like a lightning bolt. I went home and drank another bottle, and when I was done, I threw it under the couch. It made a clank, so I pushed further wondering what the noise was, and I heard more clanks. At that point, I moved the couch, and there were thirty empty pints of booze hidden underneath. I realized I'd been drinking there every night, shoving the bottles under and passing out. I remember counting those bottles and thinking, 'There's thirty. One for every year of my life.' The next day I checked into a hospital."

MANAGING UNCERTAINTY

Reaching new goals requires making a change, and change requires that we take risks. The most important ingredient for successful risk taking is the willingness to try something without being sure of the outcome. Although assessing your situation before taking action is useful, it can only help minimize the risks not eliminate them. To reach your goals, you therefore must be willing to move forward in spite of whatever uncertainty remains. When Roland Pelletier accepted this principle, he took the first steps toward recovery.

When he entered the alcohol rehabilitation program, Roland was completely unsure of himself and his situation. He did not know if he could last the full thirty days or if he could even survive without drinking. Yet he persevered, allowing himself to experience uncertainty day by day in order to reach his goal.

Most of us react to uncertainty by trying to control. Control, we believe, will enable us to manage the risks more effectively, thereby enhancing the possibility of success. In fact, just the opposite is true. The more you try to control the less control you have. The most effective way to manage uncertainty is to gather as much information as you can and then to let go and trust that you will achieve the best possible outcome. Letting go and trusting enabled Roland Pelletier to complete his recovery program and take charge of his life.

When Roland stopped drinking, he stopped trying to control the world around him. No longer did he rely on alcohol to help him create an "amusing" personality in order to make people like him. Instead, he simply was who he was, and he realized that some people would respond positively to him and others would not.

"For years," he explained, "I used alcohol to make people like me. Drinking helped me feel funny and sociable. Without a drink, I felt awkward and silly and insecure. I finally accepted that other people don't make me feel silly, that I choose to feel that way. I realized that I can choose to sit alone and not have any fun because of my fears, or I can set the fear aside and go out and dance and have a good time.

109

"Self-control is healthy," he continued, "but too much control is not. There is a difference between taking charge of your life, taking responsibility for what happens to you, and trying to control your environment to make things happen. That just doesn't work. You have to be flexible and trust that things will happen, and then they do. If you control people, you lose them. Then you have to start all over by looking inside and taking the controlling self out."

Accepting responsibility for his attitudes and decisions empowered Roland to make the changes necessary to leave alcohol behind. He realized that blaming others only made him feel helpless because it put them in control of his life. The more powerless he felt the more he struggled to control people with his drinking. The moment he broke this cycle he took his first steps toward taking charge of his life. He slowly realized that although he could not control the people and events around him, he could control his attitude. By changing his attitude, he changed his self-perception and his life.

"When I stopped drinking," he explained, "I found that the world doesn't go away just because the bottle does. There is still gossip, politics and taxes. You have to eat, sleep and clothe yourself. I learned I couldn't control people, places or things, but that I had to change my own thinking about what was around me. I discovered that I can be part of the problem or part of the solution—by taking charge of myself, my attitudes and what I do."

THINK POSITIVELY

The key to successful risk-taking is a positive mental attitude. All of us fall into negative thinking some of the time. However, it is possible to change our negative minds at any moment and replace negative thoughts with positive ones. The best way to do this is to recognize the three most common negative refrains—"Yes but . . . , If only . . . , What if . . . ?"

110

–and to stop using them. When was the last time you repeated one of these phrases? How often do you use them as an excuse to avoid risk?

Your thinking shapes your behavior which in turn shapes your life. Roland Pelletier thought he was awkward and unattractive, and he behaved as if this information were true. He drank to hide his insecurity and to feel better about himself. Drinking, in turn, destroyed him physically, mentally and spiritually, and, as his little niece so directly noted, it ultimately made him sick and unattractive. He essentially became what he thought.

When Roland started giving himself the three A's—approval, acceptance, appreciation—his self-perception changed, and soon he was replacing negative thoughts with positive ones. Instead of saying to himself, "What if that pretty woman won't dance with me?" he started thinking, "I'd like to dance with her. If she doesn't want to dance with me, I'm still OK. I'll ask someone else." As his thinking changed, his behavior changed as well. He decided to go dancing for the pure fun of it without worrying how other people would respond.

As Roland Pelletier's story shows, your mind is only as good as the thoughts that dominate it. If you choose to focus on fear and negativity, your life will be negative and you will have trouble realizing your goals. Real courage demands that we stop making excuses and start taking the steps necessary to achieve our dreams. When Roland decided to stop drinking, he stopped asking, "What if . . . ?" Instead, he checked into a hospital and started moving toward sobriety step by step.

You, like Roland Pelletier, are capable of replacing negative thinking with a positive mental attitude. You have the ability to stop worrying about the things in the future you cannot change and to take the risks necessary to realize your goals. Worrying keeps you from being your best; it helps

111

you avoid change; it takes time and energy away from positive endeavors; it paralyzes and keeps you immobile.

In managing the risks associated with reaching your goals, make a commitment to eliminate worry from your thinking. Write down your greatest concerns and deepest fears about implementing your goals and put them in a jar. Then set aside one hour a week to read over all the worry notes you have written. Spend the full hour worrying. Ask yourself, "What's the worst thing that could happen here? How could I handle that?" Then burn all your worries for the week and start again if you need to.

MOMENT TO MOMENT

The day Roland Pelletier decided to stop drinking he also decided to let go of the past, accept the present and stop worrying about the future. He realized that he could not change what had already happened but that he could learn from it and move on. "The most important factor in breaking out of a bad situation," he noted, "is recognizing it is bad and then forgetting about it. There is nothing you did yesterday that you can change, but you can change today. When I decided to go to the hospital, my first goal was just to make it there. Once I was in, I wanted to finish the thirty-day program, but I wasn't sure I could do it. There was a nurse there who told me, 'Just take today. You're alive, you're here. Forget what's past and what's out there in the future. Protect your life and get through today.'

"Most of us are afraid of risk," he continued, "but our fear is a vehicle of procrastination. When I live in fear, I live in yesterday because the situation is familiar and reminds me of past insecurities. When I'm afraid, I sit down and ask myself why. It's usually because I'm projecting my past experiences into the future. Yesterday is gone, it's history. There's nothing I can do to change it except learn what my fears were and let them go.

"When an old tape comes in," he concluded, "I can react to that tape and let it distort the present situation. Or I can let the tape play itself out and then say to myself, 'I have a decision to make. Do I feed the tape, or do I do what is best for me at the moment?' Failure is putting yourself in the future and saying why you can't do something before you try. When I do the best I can today, moment by moment, then I have succeeded."

As Roland's story so clearly illustrates, we all have the power to control our own lives. We can choose at any moment to let go of the past and live in the present moment. We can choose to see each moment anew with all its possibilities for joy, fulfillment and positive growth. Or we can choose to be paralyzed and controlled by old, negative experiences. Taking a risk means seeing each challenge with new eyes. It requires that we let go of our old fears and move into new territory without being sure of what we will find there.

For some of us, this may simply involve doing something alone, like going to a movie or taking a walk out in the sunlight. For others, it may mean meeting a new physical challenge such as rock climbing, sailing or skiing. For others still, it may be changing careers, going back to school or starting a business. Whatever your goal, it will require that you let go of the past–past negativity, past failures, past fears–and look at the risks involved through new eyes. The following two exercises will help you move through this process.

HELLO/GOOD-BYE

Divide a piece of paper into three sections. Write "Good-bye" at the top of one section, "Hello" at the top of the second, and "Thank you" at the top of the third. Think for a

113

moment of all the things in your life you want to leave behind as you work to achieve your new goals and say "Good-bye" to them. These may be attitudes, fears, habits, things, relationships, or anything else. Write them under "Good-bye."

Now think about the things you want to greet as you put your goals into effect. Write them under "Hello." Visualize each item as you write it. Finally, think about the things in your life for which you are most grateful. Note these under "Thank-you." Feel as much gratitude as you can for what you already have. This exercise will help you eliminate old, negative elements from the past and generate new, positive ones to replace them.

DELIVER THE LETTER

Once a month write yourself a letter. Tell yourself all the positive things you have done especially in terms of reaching your goal. Give yourself praise and appreciation for your accomplishments. Be careful to avoid criticizing yourself for not moving fast enough or for failing to do something you think you should have done. Avoid the words should, ought to, must, can't. Keep your letters in a folder or notebook and go back and read them all from time to time. (Thanks to Roland Pelletier for this suggestion)

Meeting The Challenge Of Risk

The challenge of risk is the challenge of self-trust; it is the challenge of opening your life to new possibilities, new people and new growth. For many of us, risk-taking is a little frightening. However, once we learn to trust ourselves and our decisions, our fear will diminish and our confidence will grow. You are capable of making this choice at any moment. You have the power within to take charge of your life and direct its course. This includes the power to assess and then take risks.

Decide right now to think positively about risk, about yourself, about your life, and take the first step toward realizing your goals.

I accept this challenge.

_____   _____

Name   Date

CHAPTER SEVEN

WHAT ELSE DO I NEED TO DO

Force has no place
where there is need of skill.
– Herodotus

"Genesis, Exodus, Leviticus, Numbers, Deuteronomy"–
I hear a child's voice repeating each long, Biblical name
clearly and without hesitation. I see myself, nine years old
and about to complete my first speaking engagement–reciting
the books of the Bible before my friends at Church. I am
wearing a blue dress and my best shoes. Two long blonde
braids form straight arrows down my back, softened by the
blue silk bows tied at their tips. I am standing as straight as
the braids, my shoulders square, my head high and my eyes
on the children seated in front of me. In spite of the long
words, I am smiling and appear at ease.

Even as a child, I wanted to be a speaker. My family
called me "Sarah Bernhardt" because I loved being on center
stage. I joined the youth group at our church because I
wanted opportunities to perform. However, my goals
gradually changed. By the time I finished college, I no longer

thought about performing. I majored in education because teaching was a good career to combine with marriage. Later I transferred my classroom skills into a sales and training position with Mary Kay Cosmetics. My work there allowed me to motivate others through speaking, but I still was not doing what I really wanted.

When I was forty-four, I decided to leave Mary Kay and fulfill my life dream. I realized then something I had known instinctively at age nine–I belonged in front of a group. Speaking was what I loved, and speaking was what I should do. At that moment, I decided to change careers and become the successful speaker I had always wanted to be.

Deep inside, all of us know what is best in our lives, yet we often ignore our inner voice. Instead of following the path we <u>want</u> to follow, the one that gives us the most joy and satisfaction, we choose the one we think we <u>should</u> follow. We simply do not believe we can have what we want. "That's a great idea," we say, "but I can't do it because...I don't have the money. I never went to college. I don't have the right skills. I'm not smart enough, tall enough, short enough, good enough." Struggling with these barriers, we lock ourselves into a negative cycle and prevent ourselves from fulfilling our life dreams.

For many years, I was unable to accept either my talent as a speaker or my need to speak. As a result, I remained in jobs that were only partially satisfying. However, once I allowed myself to pursue what I truly loved, I achieved greater success than I ever had before. The joy and exhilaration I felt inside enabled me to overcome any initial nervousness I felt about making such a radical life change. In addition, I rediscovered a principle that I seemed to know naturally as a child: Act as if, and it will become.

When I stood up to recite those long Biblical names, I was terrified. What if I forgot something? What if I made a mistake? What if I looked stupid in front of my friends? My mouth was dry, and sweat was pouring down my chest, but in spite of my fear, I kept going. By standing tall and straight, smiling and looking directly at my young audience, I projected such confidence that I actually started feeling confident. This was a technique I learned to apply again later in life.

When I started my business, I thought to myself, "I'll simply act as if I'm already successful, and then I will become successful." By acting in a confident manner, I became more confident. The more confident I was, the more seminars and speeches I booked. And the more I spoke, the better speaker I became. I envisioned myself addressing larger and larger audiences, and soon my goal was to speak before a group of five-thousand people.

Toward the end of my first year in business, I was invited to present the keynote address at the yearly convention of the National Association of School Boards in Minneapolis. The program chairperson picked me up at the airport, and we were driving toward our hotel when he turned to me and said, "By the way, Charlene, I don't know if anyone told you, but there will be about five thousand people in the audience tomorrow. I hope that's OK." Five-thousand people–I had reached my goal. The speech I gave that night was the best of my career.

The way we see ourselves is the way other people see us. When we feel strong and confident inside, we project strength and confidence in our external behavior. The first step to developing a positive self-image is increasing our internal feelings of self-worth. In the beginning of this book, you learned techniques to help you do this. The next step is to learn how to project that inner confidence. On the following pages, you will discover the secret of positive self-projection. You will learn how to consciously change your behavior so that, even in moments of self-doubt and uncertainty, you will appear confident, calm and in control of the situation. By mastering the ten skills described below, you will become the confident person you are capable of becoming.

PROJECTING CONFIDENCE: TEN CRITICAL SKILLS

Skill One: Smile

When you interact with others, greet them with a smile. An open, friendly expression invites cooperation and good will. Look in the mirror and say "Hello" to yourself. The first time you do this, keep an expressionless face. Then say "hello" again and smile. Is the tone of your voice different? Do you feel different? How would you respond to yourself in each instance?

It is a rare occasion when a smile is not appropriate. Whether you are asking for information, requesting a favor, attending a class, giving directions, having an interview or even offering criticism, smiling sets a positive tone for the interaction. A friendly smile indicates receptivity and good will, thereby opening channels of communication.

Skill Two: Shake Hands

An extended hand is a sign of openness and mutual acceptance. It does not matter if you are male or female, be the first to reach out your hand. Shaking hands allows for direct physical contact which in turn communicates significant information to both parties. Is the handshake firm or limp? Does the person make eye contact along with offering his or her hand? What else can you learn from touching hands?

During the last presidential election, a friend of mine worked as the driver for one of the leading candidates. When the candidate came to the University of New Hampshire to give a speech, my friend arranged for me to meet his party at the stage door. The candidate walked up to me with a strong

119

gait, extended his hand and smiled. A newspaper reporter quickly took our picture as I smiled in return. Later that evening, the reporter called the local headquarters to ask my name. Because the candidate approached me so purposefully and shook my hand, the reporter assumed I was an important state official whose name should be included in the photo caption. Although I held no political office, at that moment the presidential candidate treated me as if I were the most important person in the state.

Skill Three: Touch

Touching adds impact to your words and makes people feel as if you really care. It closes the distance between you and the person to whom you are talking. Think about your own experiences. To what extent do the interactions when someone reached out and touched you stand out? How were these interactions different from those when open space remained between you and the other people involved?

Skill Four: Listen

When you are engaged in a conversation, how often do you find your attention wandering? Sometimes we hear only a few words of a conversation because we are worrying about something else–paying bills, meeting deadlines, going to the doctor or some other pressing matter. Occasionally, we think we know what the person is going to say next or we start planning our response to what we have already heard. In all these instances, our minds are not focused on the conversation, and we often miss what is really being said.

There are several techniques that will help you become a better listener. Look at the speaker's face, watch his or her expression and note what is being said nonverbally. Ask questions occasionally. This will require that you pay close attention to the speaker's words. Repeat what you have heard in summarizing statements. This will encourage the speaker to expand on his or her views as you indicate your understanding of the conversation. You will learn surprising things about others if you listen carefully. You also will find that they start listening more attentively to you.

Your eye-contact is important as well. A good listener shows attention and interest through strong eye contact; however, prolonged staring can be interpreted negatively. When speaking, break eye contact as thought requires, but remember that looking away at critical moments can be interpreted as an indication of untruth or uncertainty. During a business conversation, imagine there is a triangle on the other person's forehead and direct your gaze there. This creates a serious atmosphere, and your partner senses you mean business. When your gaze drops below the other person's eye level, a social atmosphere develops. The triangle is now between the eyes and the mouth. Moving your eyes lower creates a sense of intimacy. When the triangle drops between the eyes and the chest, this suggests a feeling of personal closeness.

Skill Five: Use Positive Gestures

Dr. Albert Mehrabian of UCLA has done extensive research to determine how people project themselves nonverbally. He found that 55 percent of our communication is done visually and that the visual impression we create easily overrides the words we say. Even our tone of voice weighs more (38 percent) than the actual content of our conversation. Only 7 percent of what we communicate is done verbally. How you look, act and sound is therefore far more important to the listener than your actual words.

People notice your posture first, immediately followed by your bearing and the way you walk. Erect posture with an energetic gait shows confidence while slumped shoulders,

121

dragging feet and a tendency to lean against walls and furniture indicate insecurity.

By using your arms and body in a particular manner, you can create either a hostile or a receptive atmosphere. When people have a nervous, negative or defensive attitude, they fold their arms firmly on their chests, a strong signal that they feel threatened. Should you encounter an arms folded stance, try to get those persons to uncross their arms. Hand them something, ask them to lean forward and listen to you, or to show you where something is or how it works.

Open arms, exposed palms, leaning forward and head tilting are all positive signals. When others use these gestures, we feel that they enjoy our company, and we start enjoying theirs. Using these gestures also helps you influence others toward your point of view. In contrast, crossed arms, body and head turned away, side glances, head down, eyebrows turned down all show disapproval or even hostility. Hands clasped behind the head indicate a superior attitude. Remember, the opening up of the body suggests a positive, receptive attitude while crossing the body is a negative sign.

The way you dress also communicates who you are. For women, dark suits and dresses with long skirts suggest more authority than soft, floral patterns. Men should wear crisply starched shirts and neckties that reach the waist. Both should avoid short sleeves and strive for a layered look–jackets, vests, sweaters worn over blouses and shirts. Light colors make you appear more approachable and friendly; bright colors more outgoing and dynamic; and color combinations which are high in contrast send a confident, powerful message.

The style and fit of your clothing plus the color you are wearing should agree with your verbal communication. What you wear should be based on your relationship with the people you are about to see or the position you wish to take in the relationship. However, the outside must balance with the inside or the clothes will be perceived as little more than a facade. Clothes can heighten your presence but they cannot take the place of a positive attitude.

Skill Six: Communicate Your Thoughts And Feelings Clearly

People cannot respond to you if you do not tell them what you want, need or feel. Make your expectations clear and ask others what they expect. Assume nothing. I remember one seminar participant who shared the following observation. She told the group, "Assume makes an 'ass' out of 'u' and 'me'." We can avoid misunderstandings simply by asking questions to clarify what we have heard.

Sometimes we feel frustrated because people seem to be working against us. Working at cross purposes is almost always caused by miscommunication. When you state your goals, plans and wishes clearly, then it is easier to reach a consensus on what course of action to follow. Otherwise, you feel misunderstood.

Your tone of voice is also important. The deeper and stronger your voice, the more secure and self-assured you sound. The higher and more faltering the voice quality, the less confident you appear. Men have a built-in advantage here. Women often have to work on developing a lower tone. Remember that people relate well to those who sound like they do. If you are a Northerner visiting the South, slow down your speech. Someone from Texas speaking with a New Yorker might move the conversation a little more quickly.

Skill Seven: Involve People

Creating positive change is one theme of this book. Setting and achieving new goals is one way to implement change in your life. However, when you decide to do something different, that decision affects the lives of other

123

people. This is true whether the desired changes occur in your personal or work life, or both. If you want your family and co-workers to support your goals, then it is important that you communicate clearly to them how those goals will affect them.

When people are involved in decisions that affect them, they are more willing to carry out the decisions made. If you try to impose change on others without their input, you will meet with suspicion and resistance. Ask the important people in your life their[opinions] about the changes you hope to make. What impact do they see these changes as having? What is the best way to implement the desired change? How does your new path affect them and how do they feel about this? What information do they need to help you effect the changes smoothly? What do they fear and how can you address these fears? Taking the time to answer such questions will build enthusiasm and trust. By making other people a part of the change process, you will reach your goals with a minimum amount of stress.

Skill Eight: Recognize, Respect And Support Others

As you move toward your goals, you will need the support and assistance of the people around you—your family, co-workers and friends. We do not work in a vacuum but rather need others to help us turn our dreams into reality. One of the most effective ways to improve your personal interactions is to recognize other people for what they have done. When we lack confidence in ourselves, we often show this by attacking and criticizing others. Yet such behavior only imposes barriers between people, making the journey toward our goals only more difficult.

Sometimes it is necessary to find ways to correct or change a given situation. When this occurs, focus on the problem, not the personality, of the person involved. Work to

generate solutions rather than concentrating on who is at
fault. By offering encouragement and support, you will create
an atmosphere of enthusiasm and good will. You will also
help others to build the confidence they need to get the job
done.

When you have reached a new objective and are closer to
your goal, thank those around you for their help. People
cannot know when you are pleased if you do not tell them.
Express your appreciation verbally, in writing or even with a
small gift. Thank your spouse, children or relatives for their
support; show gratitude to your co-workers or your boss for
their assistance; and remember anyone else who has assisted
you in breaking the barriers you encountered as you worked
to achieve your goals.

Remember that all of us have four basic human needs:
empathy, cooperation, recognition and respect. The more we
fulfill those needs, both for ourselves and others, the more
empowered we become. Empowerment is accompanied by a
sense of security and well being that forms the basis for
purposeful action. Purposeful action in turn moves us toward
our goals. However, most of us at one time or another
experience confusion around these four needs. Instead of
giving and receiving empathy, cooperation, recognition and
respect, we are driven by a desire for sympathy, power, fame
and prestige. We repeatedly try to manifest these four things
in our work life and in our personal relationships. Yet even if
we achieve a measure of each, we do not feel satisfied
because our basic needs still remain unfulfilled. In an effort
to alleviate our discomfort and get what we need, we simply
repeat this negative cycle.

Roland Pelletier, the recovering alcoholic you met in the
last chapter, offers a good example. Driven by his insecurity,
Roland wanted power and control over other people to make
himself feel better. He believed that by being sociable and

amusing he could make people like him. He sought prestige by buying drinks for everyone in the bar, by inviting acquaintances out to fancy restaurants, by driving expensive cars and wearing expensive clothes. Yet fulfilling these desires did not bring him inner strength and self-acceptance. On the contrary, he found that power and prestige were illusory and that his greatest source of strength lay in self-respect.

Similarly when Jeanette Smith returned home from her year of rehabilitation, people thought she wanted sympathy. Their attitude was, "Poor Jeanette. She's had such a hard time. She's handicapped. We have to treat her differently." However, what Jeanette really wanted was empathy and cooperation. She needed people to understand what she had experienced and to feel what she was feeling: isolated, frustrated and rejected. To ease her transition back to school, she also needed the respect and support of her teachers and fellow students.

Skill Nine: Accept Others

All of us have expectations both of ourselves and of others. When we impose those expectations on the people around us, we inevitably will be disappointed. No one can live up to our ideals all of the time. In fact no one should have to fulfill our expectations at any time whatsoever. Effective relationships are based on acceptance of people for who they are. However, such clarity of vision is difficult to achieve. We view others through the lenses of our expectations, and the image we see is often distorted.

We may expect a spouse to fulfill our romantic ideal, a co-worker our image of dedication, ourselves a high standard of perfection. It is impossible for anyone to fulfill such expectations. Cooperation and support are based on mutual acceptance and the clear expression of needs and desires.

Skill Ten: Accept Yourself

Self-acceptance is the first skill you worked to develop when you started this book. It is the most difficult one to achieve and the most important. It forms the basis for self-confidence and helps build self-esteem. Once you accept yourself for who you are, you stop comparing yourself to other people. In such comparisons, you tend to compare your weaknesses to other's strengths, and invariably you emerge the loser. Instead of dwelling on what you lack, look at your skills and abilities honestly and start building on what you already have. The following exercise will help you do this.

Sit for a moment, take a few deep breaths and relax. Then look back over your life and think about everything that you have accomplished. Spend five or ten minutes remembering some of the high points. What were these moments? How did you look? How did you feel? What had you accomplished? Be sure to include accomplishments from every era: childhood, adolescence, young adulthood, up to the present moment. Remember athletic achievement, hobbies, special accomplishments at home and community service as well as career or academic achievements.

As you look back over your life history, think about the different challenges that you encountered. How did you meet these challenges? What skills were required and how did you develop them? Now make a portrait of yourself that embodies all the skills you have developed. This can be a word-picture, a figure drawing, a painting–anything that expresses you in terms of your life accomplishments. When you finish this exercise, you will be astonished by what you see: a highly skilled person who has already achieved many goals.

Your life story shows that you are a person of strength and ability. By giving yourself credit for what you have done, you will increase your confidence. This in turn will enable you to meet new challenges and reach new goals. As you consciously change your attitude toward yourself, you will generate a positive cycle. Confidence leads to success, and success generates more success, which, in turn, builds self-esteem. Self-acceptance is the final and most important skill that you need in order to achieve your goals.

Challenge

Become the confident person you are capable of becoming by developing the Ten Skills. Practice each skill at least once daily and watch your confidence grow.

I accept this challenge.

_____   _____

Name   Date

CHAPTER EIGHT

BLUEPRINT FOR CHANGE

All our dreams can come true
—if we have the courage to pursue them.
— Walt Disney

Walt Disney was a man with a wonderful imagination and a wonderful dream, yet he was not just a dreamer. He had the courage and the ability to transform his vision into a magic reality that still delights the world. In my work as a teacher, trainer and speaker, I have learned that every person has a creative imagination and a private dream, and every person has the ability to bring that dream to life. The most challenging thing for all of us is to take those first steps toward making our dreams come true. In Disney's words, we need the courage to pursue what we most want.

In my seminars I have noticed that people love to talk about their dreams. Sharing our hopes with others makes us feel one step closer to actualizing our vision and achieving our goals. Yet there is an enormous difference between talking about what we want to do and actually doing it. Sometimes when we spend an hour or two daydreaming out loud, we feel as if we have already accomplished what we hope to do. Because we have directed considerable verbal attention toward our goals, we have the illusion that we are well on the way to reaching them.

Sharing hopes and dreams is helpful and fun, but there comes a time when we need to stop talking and start doing. This is the point you have reached in the change process. Throughout this book, you have thought about yourself and your life dreams. You have identified the barriers that stand between you and fulfilling those dreams. You have learned how to break those barriers and make your dreams come true. Now is the time for action.

On the following pages you will find your personal Blueprint for Change. The Blueprint is a six-step process that will enable you to take the concrete actions necessary to achieve your goals. It is designed especially to help you bring your dream to life.

MY PERSONAL BLUEPRINT FOR CHANGE

Step 1: The Present Moment: Where Am I Now?

Write a few sentences describing your present situation

1. My personal life (family, living situation, spiritual life, health)_____

_____

_____

2. My financial situation _____

_____

3. My career _____

_____

4. Other _____

_____

Possible changes I would like to make _____

_____

_____

Step 2: My Future, My Dream: Where Am I Going?

1. What is my future goal?_____

_____

2. What does my goal look like (picture, sketch, written description)?

3. Why do I want this goal? _____

_____

4. Where am I now with regard to my goal? _____

_____

5. What barriers stand between my goal and me? _____

_____

6. How can I overcome these barriers? _____

_____

7. When will I do this? _____

_____

Step 3: Means To An End: How Will I Get There?

1. What do I need to help me reach my goal (training, advice, money, information)? _____

_____

2. Where can I find the necessary resources? _____

_____

3. Who can help me (name, address, phone)? _____

_____

Step 4: Sometime Is No Time: When Will I Start?

Steps To Reach My Goal   **Date To Start**

_____   _____

_____   _____

_____   _____

_____   _____

Three/Six/Nine Month Progress Report

_____

_____

_____

Necessary Revisons In My Action Plan

_____

_____

_____

Step 5: Problems, Problems: What About The Unexpected?

1. Potential problems I foresee _____

_____

_____

2. How will I handle these problems? _____

_____

_____

_____

Step 6: What Is My New Life Like?

Imagine the date to be one year from now. Write a letter to a friend or family member. Describe what you have achieved over the past year as if you had already done it. Use the past tense and include information about what goals you have reached and how you reached them. Then write about your new life as if it were a reality. Use the present tense. What are you doing? What is your life like? How do you feel?

CONCLUSION

With your Blueprint for Change in hand, you are now ready to move toward your dream. You have acquired the courage, the energy, the vision and the practical information needed to reach your goal. Although this book may have helped you, these pages alone could not have brought you to this point. You deserve congratulations and applause for your efforts, your commitment and your dedication to change. As Nancy Wilson Ross wrote many years ago,

> No one saves us but ourselves;
> No one can and no one may,
> We ourselves must walk the path,
> Teachers merely show the way.[1]

Whether you are preparing to take your first step or are re-evaluating your progress in midstream, I wish you success. You, too, can walk the path and **absolutely** achieve whatever you set out to do.

[1] Nancy Wilson Ross, "The Return of Lady Brace," (New York), Random House, 1987, page 146.

BIBLIOGRAPHY

Aberti, Robert E. and Michael L. Emmons. Stand Up, Speak Out, Talk Back. New York: Pocket Books, 1975.

Bennes, Warren and Burt Nanus. Leaders: The Strategies for Taking Charge. New York: Harper & Row, 1985.

Bettger, Frank. How I Raised Myself from Failure to Success Through Selling. Englewood Cliffs, NJ: Prentice-Hall, 1949.

Carnegie, Dale. How to Win Friends and Influence People. New York: Simon & Schuster, 1981.

Calero, Henry and Gerard I. Nierenberg. How to Read a Person LIke a Book. New York: Pocket Books, 1973.

Conklin, Robert. How to Get People to Do Things. Chicago: Contemporary Books, 1982.

Covey, Stephen R. 7 Habits of Highly Effective People. New York: Simon & Schuster, 1989.

Dyer, Dr. Wayne W. Pulling Your Own Strings. New York: T. Y. Crowell Co., 1978.

_____. The Sky's the Limit. New York: Simon & Schuster, 1980.

Garfield, Charles A. Peak Performance. New York: Warner Books, 1984.

Gawain, Shakti. Creative Visualization. San Rafael, CA: New World Library, 1978.

Greene, Susan D. and Melanie C. L. Martel. The Job Hunter's Guide. Manchester, NH: Sterling Communicaitons Ltd., 1990.

Hennig, Margaret and Anne Jardim. The Managerial Woman. Garden City, NY: Anchor Press/Doubleday, 1977.

Hill, Napoleon. Think and Grow Rich. New York: Fawcett Crest, 1960.

_____. You Can Work Your Own Miracle. Greenwich, CT: Fawcett Publications, 1971.

Hunsaker, Phillip and Anthony J. Allesandra. The Art of Managing People. Englewood Cliffs, NJ: Prentice-Hall, 1980.

Iacocca, Lee A. Talking Straight. Toronto, NY: Bantam, 1988.

Mandino, Og. The Greatest Miracle in the World. New York: Frederick Fell Publishers, 1975.

Peck, M.D., M. Scott. The Road Less Traveled. New York: Phoenix Press, 1985.

Peters, Thomas J. Thriving on Chaos. New York: Knopf-Random House, 1987.

Schuller, Robert. Move Ahead with Possibility Thinking. New York: Jove/HBT Books, 1978.

Tannen, Ph.D., Deborah. You Just Don't Understand. New York: William Morrow & Company, Inc., 1990.

Vogt, Judith F. and Kenneth L. Murrell. Empowerment in Organizations. San Diego, CA: University Assoc., Inc., 1990.

Wilkens, Joanne. Her Own Business: Success Secrets of Entrepreneurial Women. New York: McGraw-Hill, 1988.

136

CHARLENE SHEA, CSP
A Dynamic, Energetic Speaker

Charlene Shea is considered by many to be a leading spokeswoman in the field of Positive Change, Motivational Thinking, Diversity, and Human Resource Development. She has an uncanny ability to translate complex theories into practical, useful techniques that people in every walk of life can understand and utilize immediately.

Her timely topics include:
Managing Workplace Diversity
Look–Your Body's Talking
Absolutely! You Can Create Positive Life
Changes
Taking the Strain Out of Stress

If you'd like to have Charlene speak at your next meeting or conference, or if you would like to discuss tailoring a seminar to your specific group, you may write to her at:

121 Allied Street
Manchester, NH 03109

or call
(603) 668-7016
or 1-800-843-1300, Ext. 720